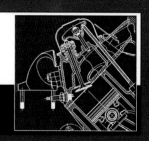

MUSCLE CARS
IN DETAIL   No. 10

1970 *Plymouth*
ROAD RUNNER

Scott Ross

CarTech®

CarTech®

CarTech®, Inc.
838 Lake Street South
Forest Lake, MN 55025
Phone: 651-277-1200 or 800-551-4754
Fax: 651-277-1203
www.cartechbooks.com

© 2018 by Scott Ross

Edit by Paul Johnson
Layout by Monica Seiberlich

ISBN 978-1-61325-304-5
Item No. CT581

Library of Congress Cataloging-in-Publication Data

Names: Ross, Scott, author.
Title: 1970 Plymouth Road Runner in Detail no. 10 / Scott Ross.
Description: Forest Lake, MN : CarTech, [2017]
Identifiers: LCCN 2016041203 | ISBN 9781613253045
Subjects: LCSH: Road Runner automobile–History. | Plymouth automobile–History. | Muscle cars–United States–History.
Classification: LCC TL215.R585 R67 2017 | DDC 629.222/2–dc23
LC record available at https://lccn.loc.gov/2016041203

Written, edited, and designed in the U.S.A.
Printed in China
10 9 8 7 6 5 4 3 2 1

Front Cover: *For 1970, the Hemi Road Runner remained the most powerful engine in the lineup. Equipped with two 4-barrel carburetors, the 426 was modestly rated at 425 hp. This rare hardtop carries the 727 TorqueFlite automatic transmission, Air Grabber hood, and A32 Super Performance Axle package with 4.10 gears, and Rallye wheels with Goodyear Polyglas GT F60-15 tires. (Photo Courtesy David Newhardt)*

Frontispiece: *The Air Grabber drew in mass quantities of cool outside air for enhanced performance. Keeping the Air Grabber open not only helped the 426 on the strip, it was also an intimidating factor while the vehicle was staging next to its opponent. (Photo Courtesy David Newhardt)*

Title Page: *The 1970 Road Runner featured aggressive updated exterior styling and the best high-performance drivetrain packages that Plymouth offered, all built with Chrysler's rugged and reliable Unibody construction. For 1970, the Road Runner was offered in three body styles: hardtop, coupe, and convertible (shown). (Photo Courtesy David Newhardt)*

Contents Page: *Only 34 Road Runner convertibles were factory equipped with the 440 Six Barrel engine option in 1970, and this is 1 of 20 built with a 4-speed manual transmission. The A12 option package that joined the Road Runner's option list in the spring of 1969 added a third engine choice, the 440 Six Barrel, whose three Holley 2-barrel carburetors atop an aluminum intake manifold by Edelbrock created 390 hp. (Photo Courtesy David Newhardt)*

DISTRIBUTION BY:

Europe
PGUK
63 Hatton Garden
London EC1N 8LE, England
Phone: 020 7061 1980 • Fax: 020 7242 3725
www.pguk.co.uk

Australia
Renniks Publications Ltd.
3/37-39 Green Street
Banksmeadow, NSW 2109, Australia
Phone: 2 9695 7055 • Fax: 2 9695 7355
www.renniks.com

Canada
Login Canada
300 Saulteaux Crescent
Winnipeg, MB, R3J-3T2 Canada
Phone: 800 665 1148 • Fax: 800 665 0103
www.lb.ca

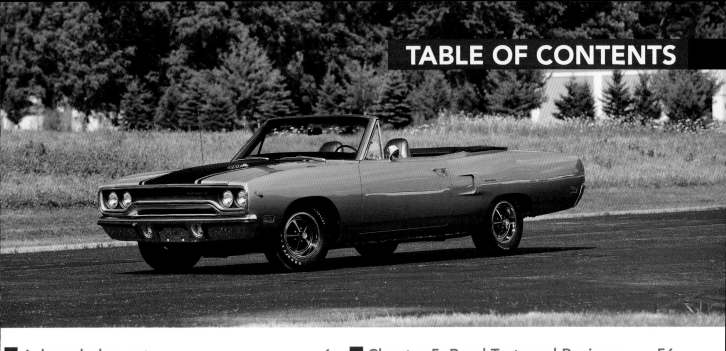

TABLE OF CONTENTS

DEDICATION

To author Scott Ross, who gave every task his all. He poured his passion, knowledge, and enthusiasm into this and each book he created. During the production of this title, Scott passed away. He will be dearly missed.

ACKNOWLEDGMENTS

For this, my second book for CarTech, my deepest thanks, once again, are due to my editor at CarTech, Paul Johnson. Just as with the book on E-Body Mopars, *The Definitive Barracuda & Challenger Guide: 1970–1974*, which was published in 2016, Paul's editing skills and encouragement while this book was being prepared were invaluable. Kudos are also due to the CarTech staff who turned the collection of sentences and the images supplied with them into the eye-catching book you're now reading.

A huge "Thank You!" to Henry Liebman, of Hollywood, Florida, whose Burnt Orange Metallic convertible is featured in these pages, as well as to Henry's friend Gary Montoya, whose In Violet 1970 Plymouth GTX was photographed at the same time.

Huge thanks also go to David Newhardt, who so graciously opened his archive and shared many wide-view and fine-detail shots of 1970 Road Runners, adding depth and style to the book's account of the third-year Bird.

Another source for images for these fine Plymouths was (where else?) Plymouth, Michigan. Vanguard Motor Sales not only has had many fine examples of the 1970 Road Runner in its inventory over the years, it also photographed them in exacting detail, including underbody details such as torque boxes, disc/drum brakes, and Hemi suspension details.

Appreciation for the 1970 Plymouth Road Runner isn't limited to the full-size car and its owners and restorers. Those of us too young to drive back then eagerly awaited Jo-Han Models' 1/25-scale kit and remember the thrill of seeing that wildly-illustrated kit box on our local hobby shop shelves. That interest and excitement remains in the scale-model-car hobby to this day, and I thank Claes Ericsson (from Bagarmossen, Sweden), Ken Schmidt (from Huntington, New York), and Kevin Wallenhorst (from North Royalton, Ohio) for sharing their images of the original Jo-Han kit. Special kudos to Tom Carter of Spotlight Hobbies in Grand Rapids, Michigan; through the message board, I contacted those three gentlemen.

In addition, my thanks to those 2015 Fall and 2016 Spring Daytona Turkey Run participants who brought their third-year Birds to those infield-filling events at the Daytona International Speedway, where I was able to capture fine-detail images.

For the cover car and some other rare and distinctive 1970 Road Runners, my deepest thanks go to Christine Giovingo at Mecum Auctions, as well as to Dana Mecum.

Reproduction-parts images were graciously supplied by these aftermarket sources, who are also due a big thank you: YearOne (Pat Staton), Auto Custom Carpets (Julie Tyson), and Auto Metal Direct (Aaron Hopkins).

Major thanks are due to all those at Chrysler Corporation who planned, styled, engineered, and built the 1970 Plymouth Road Runner at these Chrysler assembly plants: Lynch Road Assembly (Detroit, Michigan), Newark (Delaware) Assembly, St. Louis (Missouri) Assembly, and Los Angeles (California) Assembly. Thanks also to those who promoted and sold the Road Runner within Chrysler and its Chrysler-Plymouth Division, as well as to the Chrysler-Plymouth dealers across the United States who sold and serviced them way back when.

Plus a big shout-out to FCA Automobiles' historic-services crew, who graciously let me use historic Plymouth images, including the 1970 Plymouth *Rapid Transit System* brochure.

My biggest thanks go to you readers who've wanted a convenient source of information about the third-year Bird for your home reference libraries or to give to a friend or relative to grace their collections.

A personal note: During the writing of this manuscript, my mother, Patricia Kindig Ross, passed away before she had a chance to read it and offer her editorial critique. An English teacher by training and the wife of a Chrysler materials researcher (my father, Stuart T. Ross) at the time of my birth, her inspiration and support will never be forgotten. Thanks, Mom!

And, once again . . . thank you, readers!

INTRODUCTION

How did a comment from a car magazine editor evolve into a budget muscle car with a cartoon bird for a namesake?

That's the same kind of question as asking why that cartoon bird's idea of having fun is running down the road.

And, because it was the late 1960s when the first question was asked, the result was a legendary muscle car famous for its combination of high performance and low price: the Plymouth Road Runner

It combined the high-performance chassis and powertrain hardware (with which Chrysler had equipped its midsize B-Body cars since 1962) with the lowest-priced, barely trimmed 1968 Belvedere body, creating a car whose sub-$3,000 base sticker price drew buyers to Chrysler-Plymouth showrooms in search of a budget muscle car that Ford and Chevrolet did not have in their 1968 lineups.

The Road Runner was a winner in its first year, and the midyear addition of a two-door hardtop model brought in even more young, prospective buyers to Chrysler-Plymouth dealers nationwide. The final 1968 sales tally showed that these young buyers purchased about 45,000 Road Runners, and the final results at many of the nation's dragstrips showed Road Runners

The iconic Road Runner adorns the front fender.

with lots of wins in Stock and Super Stock classes from coast to coast, many of them with cars that were, or could have easily been, driven to the track!

What did Plymouth do to improve on 1968's success? It added a convertible Bird at the start of the 1969 model run. Then, in the spring of that year, it introduced an option package based on a ready-to-race 390-hp engine that cost about half of the Hemi's extra charge.

On top of that, *Motor Trend* magazine selected the Road Runner as its 1969 Car of the Year, citing its combination of high performance and low price.

The 1969 sales of more than 88,000 Birds pleased Chrysler's bean counters in Highland Park, who gave the Road Runner their blessing, as long as it continued to sell in big numbers.

Thus, for 1970, the Road Runner's list of standard features, available options, and interior and exterior colors grew even longer. In addition, other muscle Plymouths joined it to create the Rapid Transit System.

Since 1961, Chevrolet had promoted its performance-minded models, equipped with a Super Sport option package, which included bucket seats, special trim, and any available Chevy engine. In 1968 it created the Chevrolet Sports Department to showcase the Super Sports along with the Corvette and Camaro Z28. Similarly, Dodge promoted its performance cars through its Scat Pack starting in 1968.

Plymouth's Rapid Transit System was more than a "me, too" response to Chevrolet and Dodge. It included performance models on all four Plymouth vehicle platforms, from the compact A-Body Duster 340 to the full-size C-Body Sport Fury GT and Sport Fury S23, as well as the new E-Body 'Cuda and B-Body Road Runner and GTX. It had its own sales brochure and accessories catalogs, which performance enthusiasts at the time snapped up, as well as Performance Clinics by drag-race champions such as Ronnie Sox and Buddy Martin, who had conducted them since 1967, advising Plymouth drag racers about how to set up their cars for ideal on-track performance. That was in addition to

print and broadcast ads highlighting Plymouth's 1970 performance models.

If you were in the market for a new high-performance car in 1970, there was no better time to buy one. It seemed as though every new-car dealer on your hometown's Auto Row (except Cadillac) had at least one high-performance model in its lineup, and those cars were front-and-center in print, radio, and television ads for the new 1970 cars during the late summer and early fall of 1969.

Moreover, in the minds of many Mopar mavens, the Bird had it all: looks, performance, and that unique horn.

1968–1969: THE BIRD EMERGES: PERFORMANCE ON A BUDGET PLAN

Muscle cars in the 1960s were built for and marketed toward male drivers under the age of 30, the vanguard of the baby-boom generation that was now of driving age, and who now could choose new cars far different from the ones their parents hauled them around in to school, baseball practice, Scout meetings, and other activities. These new cars' engines delivered

Here's the original 1968 Road Runner logo, which appeared in black and white for that year only. By using the base Belvedere coupe body with police-car mechanicals, Plymouth was able to keep the base sticker price under $2,900.

The Road Runner's success in early 1968 led to calls for a hardtop body style, as well as option packages that dressed up the plain Plymouth with Satellite-grade interior and exterior trim items. This car features the federally mandated front-seat headrests, which became required on all new cars built and sold on or after January 1, 1969. (Photo Courtesy Mecum Auctions)

as much as 425 hp, richly textured bucket-seat or plain bench-seat interiors, and other luxurious options that included the same appearance, comfort, and convenience features that non-performance cars offered.

However, those features boosted a car's sticker price above $3,000, well beyond what many younger drivers (and potential new-car buyers) could afford.

Automotive writer Brock Yates noted this in one of his monthly columns for *Car and Driver* magazine. Around that same time, one of the crewmembers on Yates' SCCA Trans-Am team, who was just 19 years old at the time, suggested that car makers offer a stripped-down, budget version of their muscle cars. It should be one that limited frills while putting the best and strongest powertrain and chassis inside a body devoid of excess trim, with a cabin that also echoed the "no frills" theme.

Plymouth's product planners developed such a car for 1968, using their newly restyled two-door sedan body and police-car hardware under the hood and underneath the car, while leaving out fancy stripes, fake scoops, and fake-mag, full-wheel covers.

WHAT TO CALL IT?

A Saturday-morning cartoon show and the voice of its title character helped Plymouth and ad agency Young & Rubicam make up their minds.

The Road Runner Show, created by animator Chuck Jones, debuted on CBS-TV's Saturday-morning cartoon lineup in September 1966. Jones had originally created the cartoon for Warner Bros. big-screen endeavors in 1954. Later, Warner Bros. included it in its package of televised Saturday-morning cartoons that began airing

The colorized Bird appeared with the Exterior Decor Option group, which added the same trunk trim panel used on Satellite and Sport Satellite models, as well as other brightwork that wasn't available on base-series Road Runners.

The five-spoke Magnum 500 road wheel was a popular option for much of the Road Runner's production history. First offered in 1968, they were available long after the 426 Hemi and Track Pak axle packages were discontinued.

in 1962, the same year that the studio closed Termite Terrace, the building where its legendary animation department worked. Animators including Jones, Isidore "Friz" Freleng, and Robert McKimson followed the lead of fellow animators William Hanna and Joseph Barbera and opened their own studios to create the highly in-demand animated shows. Jones struck a deal with Warner Bros. to create new Road Runner cartoons, and thus the show was born.

One Saturday in the spring of 1967, a Chrysler Product Planning Department staffer heard the voice of the show's title character emanating from the suburban Detroit den where his children were watching television. (It was also something that I likely heard at the same time, being a devotee of the cartoon bird, and watching that same show every week on that same Detroit station.) The cartoon bird famously spent its time happily beep-beeping and running down the roads of a stylized American Southwest while evading the efforts of Wile E. Coyote to catch him (using the latest Acme Corporation weapons and gadgets, which never seemed to work . . . except for catching Wile E., that is).

Before you could say "Acme Super-Atomic Road Runner Catcher-Fryer," Chrysler and Young & Rubicam made a deal with Warner Bros. – Seven Arts to license the cartoon bird's likeness and sound for $50,000. (Seven Arts was the name of the studio after surviving founder and studio boss Jack Warner sold it in 1966, and it reverted back to Warner Bros. after another ownership change in 1969.)

Black-and-white stickers of Chuck Jones' creation went on the budget muscle Plymouth's doors and trunk lid, along with "Road Runner" nameplates. These were the only elements of style that the otherwise-bare-bones car had, except for the twin-scooped hood (shared with the GTX) and blacked-out version of the base Belvedere radiator grille. Plymouth developed a special horn that mimicked the "beep beep!" sound of the cartoon bird. With those items, the police-car hardware, and a choice of two engines (383 or 426 Hemi) and two transmissions (4-speed or automatic), the Plymouth Road Runner was born.

For 1969, the Road Runner hardtop was not only the best-selling Road Runner, it was also the best-selling two-door Plymouth of any kind. Options included a vinyl top and matte-black hood stripes, as well as the 426 Hemi, which powers this Road Runner hardtop. This car is one of 421 Hemi Road Runner hardtops built in 1969. (Photo Courtesy Mecum Auctions)

The base sticker price for the 1968 Road Runner coupe at the start of the 1968 model year was $2,870, which was about $500 less than a GTX hardtop's base price.

Young and not-so-rich muscle car buyers now had an alternative to penny pinching to save up for a new muscle car that cost nearly $4,000. They didn't have to scour the back rows of used-car lots and back pages of newspaper classifieds to find an affordable performance car that hadn't been beaten on (much) by a previous owner.

To say that the 1968 Road Runner was a surprise hit for Plymouth is an understatement. Demand was so high that it led to a pillarless hardtop version in early 1968, as well as Dodge's own budget muscle car, the Coronet Super Bee, which also went on sale in early 1968.

Final sales totals (per *Standard Catalog of American Cars 1946–1975*) showed 44,599 Road Runners rolling out of the assembly plants where the B-Body Plymouths were built (Newark, Delaware; Lynch Road Assembly in Detroit; St. Louis, Missouri; and Los Angeles, California). It outsold the GTX by a good margin: Sales of 29,240 Road Runner coupes for the full year and January–June sales of 15,359 Road Runner hardtops outpaced GTX's full-year totals of 17,914 hardtops and just 1,026 convertibles.

The Road Runner also received plenty of attention from Plymouth's price-class competition, which

Visual changes for the Road Runner and all other 1969 midsize Plymouths were minimal. Big, new taillights at each corner shed their built-in back-up lights, and the Bird's trunk lid didn't receive a Satellite or GTX-type metal-trim insert as an option.

The 440 Six Barrel featured three Holley 2-barrel carburetors atop an aluminum intake manifold by Edelbrock. It created a 390-hp screamer that cost about half the price of the Hemi option. (Photo Courtesy Mecum Auctions)

entered the budget muscle segment of the new-car market for 1969. Most notable was Ford, which similarly de-trimmed its midsize Torino GT fastback and two-door hardtop to create the Torino Cobra, offering the Police Interceptor 428 as its standard engine or the hotter, new-in-1968 428 Cobra Jet as the sole option.

Chevrolet still marketed its SS396 equipment as an option package on the Chevelle Malibu two-door hardtop and convertible. It also made the package available on the base Chevelle 300 Deluxe two-door sedan for 1969.

Pontiac considered powering a budget version of its GTO with a high-output 350-ci Pontiac engine. However, when Pontiac boss John DeLorean supposedly said, "Over my dead body will a 350 power a GTO," the company decided to install the latest version of Pontiac's Ram Air 400-inch V-8 into what became the Pontiac GTO Judge.

For 1969, Plymouth didn't stand pat with the Road Runner. That year, a convertible joined the lineup, the options expanded to include more of the comfort and convenience features available on regular-gas Satellites and Sport Satellites, and a third engine choice became available that spring. It was the 440 Six Barrel, a version of the 440-inch, RB big-block engine that sported an Edelbrock aluminum intake wearing three Holley 2-barrel carburetors, all under a pin-on fiberglass hood, in a package (Code A12) that left off hood hinges and hubcaps and delivered a 390-hp ready-to-race screamer for just $462.80 extra. (The Hemi, in contrast, cost an additional $813.45.)

Motor Trend magazine was so impressed that it crowned the Bird its Car of the Year for 1969, citing its combination of performance and value. An advertising campaign built around this honor, with more Chuck Jones–animated TV commercials, helped the Road Runner's image, and its sales, for the year.

How did the Road Runner do with the bean counters in Highland Park? For 1969, very well. With total-series sales of 88,415, which included 48,549 hardtops, 2,123 convertibles, and 33,743 coupes, it was the best-selling midsize Plymouth line of all. The Road Runner two-door hardtop was Plymouth's best-selling two-door car of any kind.

CHAPTER 1

NEW STYLING, NEW COLORS, NEW "SYSTEM"

The third-year Plymouth Road Runner debuted in 1970 with front-end styling that foreshadowed a major restyling of Chrysler's B-Body platform in 1971. Steel Rallye road wheels were a popular option; they are now being reproduced. (Photo Courtesy David Newhardt)

The third-year Plymouth Road Runner still retained its original character as a purpose-built stripped-down muscle car that provided exceptional performance and rugged reliability. The 1970 model was an evolution of the two previous models, so it was not substantially changed, but it did receive some important updates. Although a multitude of small improvements were made, the most noted and recognizable changes were to its interior and exterior styling.

It arrived in the nation's Chrysler-Plymouth dealers in September 1969, and Plymouth's Styling studios developed a new look inside and out to distinguish it from the previous model years. The third-year Bird wore new front fenders, rear-quarter panels, grille, taillights, and bumpers, as did its GTX/Satellite/Sport Satellite/Belvedere stablemates. They also shared a new, squared-off look front and rear, with a "center scoop" motif to the grille and rear body above the bumper. Carried over from 1969 were the coupe/hardtop roof, convertible top, and all the windows.

The Road Runner for 1970 combined that updated styling, which included simulated scoops on the rear-quarter panels and new optional Rallye road wheels on the outside, plus a new dash, Pistol Grip 4-speed shifter and high-back bucket seats, with a proven high-performance powertrain and chassis. It was all wrapped up in the strongest and lightest-weight midsize passenger car platform made in 1970.

As a member of the Chrysler B-Body family, the Road Runner used Chrysler's Unibody unit-body construction method, which "surrounds you in strength" thanks to stout structural members welded into and underneath the body.

Since 1960, using state-of-the-art computer technology, Chrysler's body engineers added structural strength to new body designs where needed, resulting in a unit-body assembly that was more resistant to flexing and bending than a conventional (body on frame) body was without the added weight of a full frame underneath the car. The resulting squeaks and rattles come from body bolts and connectors coming loose as the car ages.

Unibody, therefore, was the ideal method for constructing high-performance car bodies, such as the Road Runner's. For the severe-service applications such as the 426 Hemi, additional structural reinforcements were developed and welded in the appropriate bodies-in-white before they were made ready for primer and paint. After all, Chrysler engineered its high-volume B-Body platform to carry its full range of engines, from the standard 225 Slant Six and 318 LA series small-block V-8 to the B and RB big-blocks (the 383s and 440s) and the 426 Hemi.

The extra structural strength came from large structural subframes and crossmembers at the front and rear. One large crossmember is installed at the rear, just ahead of the rear axle and connects the two frame rails, essentially "boxing" the rails. On hardtop and coupe models, thick roof bows deliver added strength and rigidity to the roof panel. Up front, cowl panels, radiator support, and fender wells are tied together for improved strength. In addition, 426 Hemi-equipped cars received their own unique engine crossmember (the K-member), specially engineered for the Hemi's weight and to prevent its massive torque output from twisting the car's Unibody into a pretzel at full throttle.

The Unibody had been proven in thousands of Plymouths, Dodges, Chryslers, and 1967 and later Imperials that preceded the third-year Road Runner into production.

A totally new B-Body body design was in the works for 1971; 1970 marked the final year of the generation of midsize Plymouths and Dodges that had debuted for 1966.

Beyond the styling and comfort improvements, the Air Grabber cold-air induction featured a revised design and operation for the 1970 model year. The Road Runner's steel hood was changed from the parallel-twin-scoop design that was used in 1968 and 1969 to one with a large center bulge that accommodated the vacuum-operated Air Grabber scoop and the big carburetors that resided on top of the engine. A dash-mounted switch activated a servo, which raised and lowered the scoop. Once it was deployed, the shark teeth graphics (that resembled the nose art on the legendary Flying Tiger fighter planes of World War II) were clearly visible on each side, adding to the car's street credibility and increasing its intimidation factor over other car brands' attempts at cold-air induction.

The standard Road Runner engine was a high-output version of Chrysler's venerable 383-ci B-engine big-block V-8. Its cylinder heads, camshaft, and other components were borrowed from the 440 Magnum. Here, Coyote Duster artwork graces the air cleaner that was included with the optional Air Grabber hood (Code N96).

The coupe was still the most affordable Road Runner in 1970. Its sticker started at just under $3,100 and included potent high-performance hardware such as its standard 383 and heavy-duty suspension. The Dust Trail stripe along the side was a $15.55 option. Bright trim on the B-pillar denotes this car as having the Code A87 Decor Package, which added Satellite-level bright trim inside and out for an extra $81.50.

Although the Road Runner's available engine lineup remained the same for 1970, a high-performance floor-shifted 3-speed manual gearbox became the standard transmission; the A-833 4-speed and Torque-Flite automatic were offered as options. The A-833 was one of strongest as well as heaviest 4-speed manual transmissions built during the muscle car era. Through the 1960s, the A-833 was continually developed and improved upon, and by 1970 it was offered in two versions. One was known as the 23-spline version so named for the number of splines on its input shaft that was used on all but the highest-output V-8s including the 426 Hemi and 440 Six Barrel. For those

applications, the so-called "Hemi 4speed" (also known as the 18-spline version) was specified for 426 Hemi duty, and installed on the assembly line. That gearbox's strength was evident in its input shaft because the splines (and shaft itself) were thicker than those used with the 23-spline unit. Regardless of which 4-speed your Road Runner was built with, a Hurst 4-speed shifter was standard equipment from the factory, and did not need to be retrofitted immediately after the car was purchased.

Once again for 1970, the A-727 version of Chrysler's rugged TorqueFlite automatic was optional on all Road Runner engines, even the 426 Hemi. In service since

1964, and noted for its smooth shifting and reliability even under severe-service conditions, this heavy-duty automatic did not require the frequent band adjustment or other service procedures that rival automatics from Ford or General Motors required.

Similar to 1969 models, the base engine for 1970 was the special Road Runner 383, and there were just two engines on the option list: the 440 Six Barrel and the 426 Hemi. (The four-barrel-equipped 440 Magnum was GTX-only for 1970; it was not offered on the Road Runner until 1971.)

The base Road Runner 383 engine was no pedestrian station-wagon "grocery getter" 383. In fact, it shared many of its internals with the 440 Super Commando. These included high-flow cylinder heads, aggressive high-lift/long-duration camshaft and accompanying high-performance valvetrain, and improved exhaust manifolds that scavenged exhaust gases away from the engine in a way that rivaled many expensive aftermarket exhaust headers. As Chrysler's best rendition of the 383, the engine package produced 335 hp, and that's despite the fact that the compression ratio dropped from 10.0 to 9.5:1 for 1970.

The Road Runner convertible returned to the lineup for a second year in 1970. It's seen here with the Code V21 Performance Hood Paint option atop the new domed hood (the Air Grabber scoop is shown closed). The F60-15 Goodyear Polyglas tires were introduced in 1970; it was the largest tire size offered on a Plymouth up to that point. (Photo Courtesy Mecum Auctions)

A view under the hood of a Code N96 Road Runner shows the rubber seal that goes around the Coyote Duster air cleaner, sealing off hot, undressed air from the colder, denser outside air that the scoop directs into the engine for more power. The front of the seal sits where an optional air conditioning compressor would have been installed, making the Code H51 Airtemp air-conditioning option unavailable with the Air Grabber option.

Underneath the hood of this 1970 Road Runner resides the 426 Hemi, the most exclusive, valuable, and powerful engine installed in this model. As you can see, it's equipped with the N96 Air Grabber hood, Rallye Wheels, and the optional "Dust Trail" side stripes adorn the quarter panel, door, and fender. (Photo Courtesy David Newhardt)

The high-output 383-ci engine that was standard in 1968 remained for the 1970 Road Runner. This one wears aftermarket chrome valvecovers and an orange Mopar Electronic Ignition System control box on its firewall. Note the bottom of the Coyote Duster air cleaner, which fits flush with the air-scoop mechanism on the underside of the hood when the hood is closed.

The 426 Hemi was rated at 425 hp with 490 ft-lbs of torque; it was an $841.05 option. It's seen here covered with unrestored patina and an aftermarket battery next to it. This car is equipped with an Air Grabber scoop (Code N96) as well as with non-power-assisted brakes. (Photo Courtesy David Newhardt)

Redesigned for 1970, the Road Runner's all-vinyl bench seat incorporated the federally required headrests into the seatback. The taper toward the top allowed easier rearward viewing by the driver, something that Ford's also-new-for-1970 high-back bucket seats didn't have. (Photo Courtesy David Newhardt)

Another new feature for 1970 was the Rallye dash, borrowed from the Dodge Charger and featuring a standard 0-150–mph speedometer. The "Tick-Tock Tach" tachometer, which featured an electric clock at its center, was a $68.45 option (Code N85). (Photo Courtesy David Newhardt).

For an additional $14.05, the Bird's plumage included optional High Impact colors such as Lime Light (seen here), Tor Red, Vitamin C Orange, In Violet, and Lemon Twist. Another vivid shade of green, Sassy Grass Green, joined the High Impact color selection in February 1970, as did the shocking-pink hue Moulin Rouge.

In 1969, the Road Runner hardtop was the top-selling two-door Plymouth, and the nation's Chrysler-Plymouth dealers were optimistic that the 1970 version would sell strongly again. This one wears the optional paint color In Violet atop its freshened-for-1970 sheet metal, one of eight vivid colors available for an additional $14.05. (Photo Courtesy Mecum Auctions)

For many performance-car buyers, that was plenty. For others, the optional 440 Six Barrel offered more in the way of features and performance. Using the 440 Magnum as a base, the 440 Six Barrel used the same new-for-1970 thicker forged-steel connecting rods, molybdenum-filled top piston rings, and revised camshaft lift and duration that the 440 Magnum used, along with the 906 cylinder heads (so nicknamed from the last three digits of its factory casting number), which flanked a new intake manifold that was topped by three big Holley 2-barrel carburetors with mechanical linkage.

The new intake manifold was cast iron, instead of the cast-aluminum part sourced from aftermarket specialty company Edelbrock for 1969. Cost issues (namely involving the much-lower cost of cast iron compared to cast aluminum) and concerns that Edelbrock's foundry didn't have the capacity to support this option over a full model year led Chrysler to take it in-house for 1970. (Some early 1970 440 Six Barrels were built with leftover 1969 aluminum intake manifolds to use up the parts stock on hand.)

Add a slight bump in compression from 10.1 to 10.5:1 (meaning that the best available pump premium gasoline was your only fuel choice, lest your engine "knock" from lack of octane and tear itself apart inside) and the 440 Six Barrel was good for a peak of 390 hp and 490 ft-lbs of torque. It was a great performance value if you look at how much extra it cost, compared to the 426 Hemi.

The horsepower and torque numbers for the 440 Six Barrel were reached at lower engine speeds than the Hemi's, adding to the dual street/strip capability of the triple-carbed RB engine.

The 426 Hemi was Plymouth's top performer since its 1-2-3 finish in its debut at the 1964 Daytona 500, and being put on the B-Body Plymouth option list in 1966. For 1970, its camshaft was switched from a solid-lifter one to a hydraulic-lifter stick, while not losing any performance

Using the simulated scoops pressed into the 1970 Road Runner's rear quarter panels, the optional Dust Trail side stripes extended forward to the decal of the running bird on the front fender. The stripe appears to be dusty brown until light shines on it, which then reveals the stripe's reflective gold-colored material. (Photo Courtesy David Newhardt)

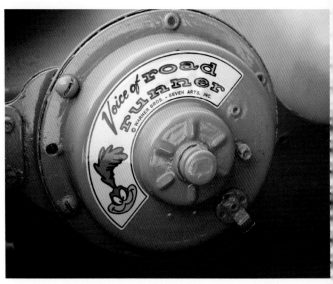

The voice of the Road Runner was the "Beep Beep!" horn that simulated the cartoon bird's voice. The purple color helped assembly-line workers tell it apart from the regular horns used on other B-Body Plymouths. The 1970 sticker still said "Warner Bros. – Seven Arts, Inc." on it, even though a 1969 studio-ownership change had shortened the name back to Warner Bros.

The 1970 Road Runner convertible shows the same vertical-pattern grille that was used on the base Belvedere and Satellite series in 1970. Also seen here is the grille's "dog bone" shape that the 1971 B-Body Plymouths wore. (Photo Courtesy David Newhardt)

as evidenced by its 425-hp rating, the same as for 1969.

The 426 Hemi resided at the top of the Road Runner's engine list and was conservatively rated at 425 hp. It carried the Bird to 60 mph in just 5.6 seconds, running the quarter-mile in 13.49 seconds.

The key feature that set the 426 Hemi apart from other big-block V-8s was its hemispherical cylinder head design. The intake and exhaust valves could flow a large volume of air efficiently through the domed combustion chamber, and the spark plug was ideally placed in the middle for efficient combustion. Born and bred to dominate drag, stock car, and other forms of racing, the "Elephant engine" (so named for its massive size and strength) had to be tamed somewhat for street service. Cast-iron exhaust manifolds and a drop in compression from 12.5:1 to a more-pump-gasoline-friendly 10.25:1 were two of the notable changes that resulted in the 426 Street Hemi for 1966, which was hand-assembled on the same special assembly line at Chrysler's Marine and Industrial Engine Plant in Marysville, Michigan, as the factory Race Hemi engines. (The 383- and 440-inch engines were built at Chrysler's Mound Road Engine Plant in Detroit, which became the company's centralized engine plant when it opened in 1958.)

Over time, Street Hemi owners wanted less to do with adjusting valve lash, and they let Chrysler's engineering crew know about it, which resulted in the hydraulic lifter camshaft that became standard in the 426 Hemi for 1970. Previous-year Hemi owners could source the new camshaft and lifters from their local Chrysler-Plymouth dealers' parts department.

As in 1969, option packages built around the ultra-heavy-duty Dana 60 rear-axle assembly were available to ensure top performance (and less parts breakage) under drag race and other severe-service conditions. For 1970, these packages became available with the 440 Six Barrel. In addition, Plymouth offered performance-axle packages built around the Chrysler 8¾-inch rear end available for 383-powered Birds, as well as TorqueFlite-equipped Hemis and 440 Six Barrels.

Inside, a new dash borrowed from the Dodge Charger provided enhanced styling and functionality. Residing in front of the driver was the Rallye gauge cluster from the GTX. It featured a big, round speedometer that went up to 150 mph, with room for an optional 8,000-rpm tachometer, an oil pressure gauge, and other gauges. An all-new Hurst Pistol Grip 4-speed manual transmission shifter handled gear selection. In the brake department, the Road Runner was fitted with 11-inch factory drum brakes that provided competent stopping power as long as the brakes didn't become too hot. To improve handling and control, heavy-duty shocks and a front sway bar kept the Bird on course.

On the outside, the term to describe the Bird was High Impact. As in colors. Vivid colors, including In Violet, Lime Light, Sassy Grass Green, Vitamin C Orange, Moulin Rouge, Tor Red, and Lemon Twist. Chrysler intended for these hot and cool colors to improve curb appeal and leave standard-hued Blue Oval and Bow Tie competitors in the dust like Wile E. Coyote. In addition, a new side Dust Trail reflective-tape-stripe option showed the cartoon bird in action, stretching from the leading edge of the front fenders across both doors to the new-for-1970 simulated scoops in each rear quarter panel.

With all that was new for 1970, plus its success record in the showroom where the Road Runner hardtop was the best-selling two-door 1969 Plymouth of all, Chrysler-Plymouth dealers had plenty of reason to be optimistic about the 1970 Road Runner.

Those dealers now had a full line of muscle cars to promote and sell, from the high-revving Duster 340, to the new 'Cuda, to the Road Runner and GTX, and all the way to the full-size Sport Fury GT and S23. This lineup was named The Rapid Transit System. Its glossy sales brochure described each performance Plymouth in detail.

Chevrolet dealers may have had their Sports Department, with their Super Sport models and Corvette Stingray, but only Plymouth had a System . . . and the Hemi on the options list!

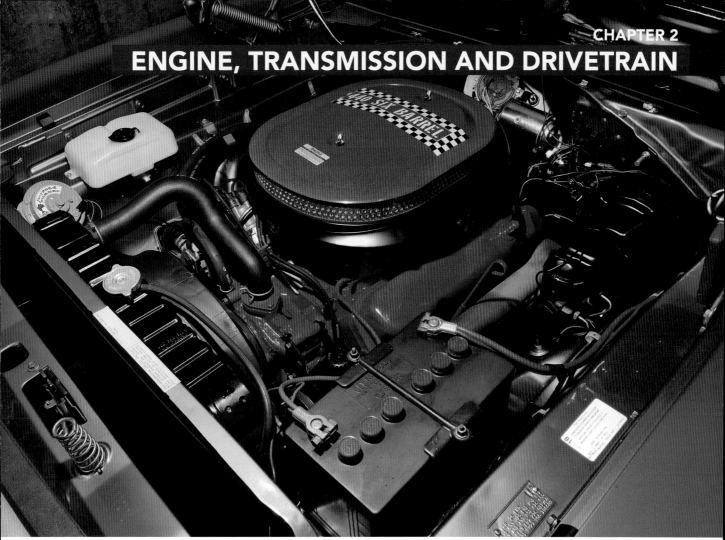

ENGINE, TRANSMISSION AND DRIVETRAIN

Optional in all Road Runners for 1970 was the 440 Six Barrel V-8. Its intake manifold was a Chrysler-made iron casting instead of an aluminum piece sourced from Edelbrock for the 1969½ version. (Photo Courtesy Mecum Auctions)

The Road Runner offered two classic wedge engines, the 383 and 440, as well as the renowned 426 Hemi engines. These engines helped establish the Road Runner as one of the most important Mopar muscle cars of all time. One indication that the Road Runner was not your average muscle car was the Rallye Instrument Cluster, with the 150-mph speedometer now standard in the revised-for-1970 dashboard. The Road Runner had plenty of power under the hood, plenty enough to spin that speedometer well into the big numbers.

383 MAGNUM

By the time the 1970 model year began, Chrysler's 383 was a known quantity. It combined advances including wedge-shaped combustion chambers and thin-wall iron-casting technology in an engine that could easily propel full-size Plymouths, Dodges, and Chryslers down the road in regular-gas form. In addition, it could transform an otherwise staid midsize Plymouth or Dodge into one with remarkable acceleration prowess.

With the 440 Six Barrel engine option, this Plymouth-specific "440+6" sticker graced the hood on either side of its stamped-in bulge, below the optional Air Grabber scoop. The term "440 Six Pack" has become the generic term for this engine. It was a Dodge-only name in 1970 and did not appear anywhere on Plymouths that were factory-built with the 390-hp engine (Code E87). (Photo Courtesy David Newhardt)

For that, you can thank the B-engine's basic design and construction, starting with its engine block and cylinder-head castings. Chrysler's powertrain engineers developed a new V-8 during the 1950s to replace three different V-8 engine series that had little parts compatibility. They chose the then-revolutionary "green-sand" method of producing iron castings using "green" (high moisture content) sand to make the casting molds, instead of the previous practice of using a drier type of sand.

From those molds, engine blocks, cylinder heads, and other components could be formed more precisely and with less iron needed to produce each piece. That in turn produced remarkably lightweight cast parts (especially the block) whose cylinder displacement matched or exceeded those of the previous Chrysler V-8s, at less cost than before. (And at much less cost than using aluminum or other light metals, whose cost per pound far exceeded that of cast iron.)

The combination of the 383-ci B engine and the Chrysler B-Body platform was well known to those seriously interested in street performance, having been a Plymouth factory powertrain combination since 1962. Many times, this combination made its presence known in the form of Plymouth's 383-powered police cars. If people were lucky, they heard the police 383 roar by; its carburetor secondaries opened up when the driver floored the accelerator pedal. If they were unlucky, they heard it from the Plymouth that was pursuing, and eventually intercepting, them.

If ever there was an incentive to keep the knowing from speeding, it was the police 383's "Don't even *think* of speeding around me!" roar. And, if those would-be evaders insisted on opening up the throttle all the way on a deserted road or completed-but-unopened freeway, the eventual failure of their engine's cast parts at high engine speeds resulted in a stream of oil and broken parts on the road and a less-than-pleased police officer whose 383-powered patrol car would be patiently idling by the side of the road as the errant driver was handcuffed, read his Miranda rights, then stuffed into the back seat.

After their patrol days were over, used police 383s, their related heavy-duty TorqueFlite automatic transmissions, and 8¾-inch rear axle assemblies were highly sought after by racers and street-performance enthusiasts. They often harvested the still-good powertrain pieces, then (many times after a simple cleanup and rebuild using new parts such as pistons and piston rings, gaskets, and fasteners) installed them in a two-door B-Body Plymouth or Dodge. The result? A competitive bracket racer that consistently ran elapsed times right at or near its "dial in" time, leading to consistent wins; or a car that was a strong runner (and regular winner) in either Stock or Modified Production classes.

This was without using a lot of expensive aftermarket parts, such as those that owners of some other competitive brands (namely Ford's 390 and Chevrolet's 396-ci big-block V-8s) needed to spend scarce dollars

The special 383, with cylinder heads and other parts "borrowed" from the 440 Magnum, was once again the Road Runner's standard engine for 1970. (Photo Courtesy Vanguard Motor Sales)

For a standard engine, the Road Runner 383 had a lot going for it, such as high-flow cylinder heads and a high-lift/long-duration camshaft. This one also sports the optional Coyote Duster cold-air induction system, which enclosed the air cleaner when the hood was closed. (Photo Courtesy David Newhardt)

Another of Chrysler's engineering advances is seen here with the electronic voltage regulator, mounted on the firewall behind the engine. A new feature for 1970, its solid-state electronic construction with no moving parts replaced the old points-style mechanical voltage regulator, and did away with high-to-low voltage swings while the engine was running. Chrysler's first Electronic Ignition System incorporated it when it was released in late 1971, and that system was standard on all U.S.-built Chrysler products for 1973. (Photo Courtesy David Newhardt)

The optional Code N96 Coyote Duster cold-air intake system sits atop this standard Road Runner 383. Note the fiberglass plenum bolted to the hood's underside. (Photo Courtesy Vanguard Motor Sales)

on to obtain the performance and durability that a stock 383 delivered.

When it came to creating the Road Runner's 383 for 1968, Plymouth could have simply chosen the existing Super Commando 4-barrel version. Rated at 330 hp and 425 ft-lbs of torque, it was the top non-Hemi engine option in non-GTX midsize Plymouths for 1967.

However, there was room for improvement, thanks to ongoing engine development during the 1960s. As a result, when the Road Runner was in the planning stages, Plymouth's product planners saw that using existing parts meant not having to specially design,

engineer, and tool up parts just for it. New tooling had added costs to what was supposed to be a "budget muscle car" engine, and quite possibly raised the base Bird's sticker price in 1968 to more than $3,000.

Foremost among the existing B/RB parts used with the Road Runner 383 were the cylinder heads used on the 440 Super Commando engine that debuted for 1967. With the same 2.08-inch intake and 1.74-inch exhaust valves as the 440 and a port design that optimized airflow at high revs over those of the 383, these heads were an instant improvement over stock 383 heads. The same goes for the 440 Super Commando's camshaft, a hydraulic-lifter stick whose .465-inch lift and 268- (intake) and 284-degree (exhaust) duration meant that it could flow the volumes of air and fuel needed to produce high-RPM power while giving the engine a fairly smooth idle, with none of the hassles of adjusting solid lifters at regular intervals, let alone after high-speed runs.

Other high-performance hardware in the Road Runner's 383 included a windage tray between the crankshaft and oil pan, which enabled a consistent oil flow and constant oil pressure to the engine's main bearings at high RPM.

Unfortunately, if you wanted air conditioning in your Road Runner, you didn't receive the Road Runner 383. Checking the H51 box on the order blank for factory-installed air conditioning not only added an "Airtemp Air Conditioning By Chrysler" decal inside the right rear window, it also included a "base" 383 in the Road Runner starting in 1968. Given that 1968 was the first year that Chrysler and the other automakers that sold cars in the United States had to comply with Federal emissions standards, low-speed engine performance, and overall drivability may have been the reason that this engine was chosen for that duty, along with scant research dollars (and time) to make the Road Runner 383 "A/C-friendly."

One thing that the Road Runner 383 had in common with all other versions of that engine, and with all

Chrysler engines of that era, was the use of drop-forged steel instead of cast iron in its crankshaft and connecting rods. Steel forgings could survive the rigors of conventional daily driving on the street. Engines used in round-the-clock taxicab service and Police use, with bursts of high-speed operation, were other instances where steel forgings lasted longer and were less prone to cracking and high-engine-speed failures than similar cast-iron parts.

Racers and hot rodders discovered that, when rebuilding a used 383 found at a salvage yard, they didn't have to spend a lot of money on aftermarket forged crankshafts and connecting rods. The stock factory parts (available through the Mopar parts network at Chrysler-Plymouth dealer parts counters) were just as durable as the aftermarket versions. They also had factory part numbers, which were essential under the rules governing production-based race classes, and where a non-stock part could lead to disqualification if discovered during a post-race inspection.

Just as significant to the 383's performance and durability was the B-engine's cylinder-head design. Chrysler's previous V-8s (especially the Chrysler Fire-Power, De Soto Firedome, and Dodge Red Ram engines) used hemispherical combustion chambers with intricate, expensive rocker gears to open and close the intake and exhaust valves. In the name of simplicity and savings, as well as durability and performance, the B-engine replaced the hemispherical combustion chambers with wedge-shaped chambers. That produced the same kind of power as did the previous engines, but at a much lower cost to produce. (Adding to the cost savings was a simplified single-rocker valvetrain with stamped-steel rocker arms, replacing the previous double-rocker setup.)

In turn, the lower cost enabled the production of the RB version of the B-engine. Short for "raised B," the RB block had a taller deck, which allowed for a longer-stroke crankshaft to be used than in the B-engine. That allowed for larger engine displacements such as the 413 ci of the first RB of 1959 and the 440-ci versions that succeeded the 413 for 1966.

For 1970, the Road Runner 383's compression dropped to 9.5:1, but its advertised horsepower (335) and torque (425 ft-lbs) were unchanged, even though no changes to its camshaft or other components were made.

440 SIX BARREL

With the Road Runner 383 as the standard engine and the 426 Hemi optional, what else could

Here's a 383-powered 1970 Road Runner with the standard 383 Road Runner engine's "pie plate" atop the air cleaner, instead of the Coyote Duster air-cleaner identification plate. (Photo Courtesy Vanguard Motor Sales)

284-degree (intake and exhaust) duration, did not come apart at high engine speeds the way some competitors' production cams did under race conditions.

The highest achievement by Chrysler's powertrain engineers crowned the engine: an aluminum intake manifold cast by Edelbrock, known for high-quality high-performance engine parts from the 1930s on, that was topped by three 400-cfm Holley 2-barrel carburetors with a progressive mechanical linkage. The design of the intake manifold meant that each carburetor was equidistant from the intake ports, which meant no high-speed fuel starvation and resulting engine damage from a too-lean air-fuel mixture.

The A12 Birds were also equipped with either a heavy-duty (18-spline) A-833 4-speed manual

Plymouth's version of the 3x2-barrel 440 was called the 440 Six Barrel, and its air cleaner wore this decal proclaiming its identity to those who opened the hood. Dodge's name for this engine option (440 Six Pack) has become the generic, if incorrect, name for it. (Photo Courtesy David Newhardt)

those seeking factory performance at a budget price want from the Road Runner?

How about an engine that put up power numbers near those of the Hemi, leading to elapsed times near those of the massive Elephant engine at around half the extra cost on the sticker?

That idea became reality in the spring of 1969, when the Code A12 440 Six Barrel option package joined the Road Runner's option list. For roughly half of the $830.65 extra tab for the Hemi, the 440 Six Barrel included the same high-RPM-ready valvesprings that were used on the Hemi; chrome-flashed valvestems, molybdenum piston rings, and a dual-point distributor, again to make the engine perform at its best at high RPM; and a low-taper camshaft and valve lifter design that, combined with a special-grind solid-lifter camshaft with .465-inch lift and

gearbox with a Hurst shifter or a column-shifted Torque-Flite that could handle the 440 Six Barrel's power. A 4.10-geared SureGrip differential and Dana 60 rear axle assembly, the stoutest in the industry, rounded out the powertrain.

Also featuring the Hemi suspension system, plain-steel 15-inch wheels with no hubcaps or wheel covers but with a set of chrome lug nuts, the A12 440 Six Barrel was ready to drive from the Chrysler-Plymouth dealer's showroom floor to the dragstrip.

Demand for this option was surprisingly high, but Edelbrock's foundry could not produce the aluminum intake manifolds fast enough to keep up. That led to a production run of 3,384 late-year 1969 Road Runners and Dodge Super Bees equipped with the A12 option, which Dodge called the 440 Six Pack.

Checking Code E87 on the order blank and adding $249.55 to the sticker price put the 440 Six Barrel under the Bird's hood. For 1970, the intake manifold was a Chrysler-sourced iron casting. Some early 1970 models may have been built with leftover 1969 aluminum intakes sourced from Edelbrock to use up the existing parts inventory. (Photo courtesy Vanguard Motor Sales)

In 1970, Airtemp air conditioning was not available with the 440 Six Barrel or with the N96 Coyote Duster hood because the hood scoop/air cleaner assembly compressor didn't clear the compressor. This Bird's owner retrofitted a smaller, later-model compressor make a Road Runner as cool inside as it is from the outside.

For 1970, Chrysler took intake manifold production in-house, and changed the material from cast aluminum to cast iron, with an eye toward keeping costs down and keeping this engine as a choice for "budget muscle car" buyers. However, during the change-over from 1969 to 1970 production, it's likely that any leftover Edelbrock intakes for the 1969 440 Six were used on early 1970 440 Six Barrels, to use up existing parts stocks.

Other updates and changes to the 440 Six Barrel for 1970 included thicker connecting rods; a new extra-heavy-duty forged-steel crankshaft that was externally balanced (the first time that a Chrysler engine had been anything but internally balanced) and its accompanying harmonic balancer; and a new passenger-side exhaust manifold with an improved heat-control valve. Two different sets of Holley 2-barrel carburetors were used for 1970: one for cars sold in California and equipped with the Evaporative Control System (ECS) that made them compliant with the Golden State's specific emissions standards, and one for the other 49 states and Canada.

On the VIN, the 440 Six was identified by the letter "V," just as in 1969.

One big factor in the 440 Six Barrel's favor: Its output of 390 hp and, more significant, the same 490 ft-lbs of torque that the 426 Hemi produced, per factory specifications. Those numbers also matched the 1969 440 Six Barrel's output.

Other changes for the 440 Six Barrel for 1970 included the 426 Hemi's valve springs, chrome-flashed valve stems, molybdenum piston rings, a dual-point ignition system, and a new passenger-side exhaust manifold that contained an improved heat-control valve. It also received what are now called "Six Pack" connecting rods: larger, thicker castings that were not only used in the 440 Six Barrel and 440 Six Pack engines for 1970, but in that year's 4-barrel 440 Magnum. Those rods' extra weight meant that an externally balanced heavy-duty

The snarling teeth on the Flying Tigers P-40 fighter planes likely inspired the decals on this open Air Grabber scoop. This car features the Code V21 Performance Hood Paint option; for $18.05 extra, it added matte black to the top of the hood bulge and alongside it.

This view of the Air Grabber scoop's underhood workings shows how much room it requires at the forward end of the engine; it takes up space where an Airtemp air conditioning compressor would reside. Those who ordered the Air Grabber option were likely interested more in power and acceleration than comfort and convenience. If they wanted a plush car with all the comfort and convenience options, they would have bought an Imperial!

crankshaft was needed; these engines used the first externally balanced crankshaft ever in a Chrysler car.

Another change for 1970 was a stamped-steel hinged hood replacing the pin-on fiberglass hood included with the 440 Six Barrel option in 1969; it was offered with an Air Grabber cold-air inlet at its center, directly over the carburetors. The Air Grabber option (Code N96) was also available with the Road Runner's 383 and 426 Hemi engines, and it permitted the car's driver to pull a vacuum-assisted switch under the dash to open it and feed more cold, dense outside air into the engine. It also showed off a set of "Air Grabber" decals on each side of the scoop that reminded some of the nose markings on the legendary Flying Tigers Curtiss P-40 Warhawk fighter planes that distinguished themselves in combat over the skies of China and Southeast Asia during World War II. Pushing in the switch closed the scoop and kept rain, bugs, and other flying contaminants out of the engine's air cleaner.

Unfortunately, if you wanted air conditioning with the Air Grabber option, you were out of luck. The scoop's

mechanism took up the space at the front of the engine where the air conditioning compressor would reside.

Another big factor was the price for the 440 Six option. It was just $249.55 extra, far less than the Hemi's $841.05 tariff, and much more in keeping with the Road Runner's "budget muscle car" character. Also, the 440 Six Barrel was available on any Road Runner for 1970 from the start of the model year onward, and not just on the coupe and hardtop as was the case in the spring of 1969.

426 HEMI

The 426 Hemi was originally an all-out race engine developed for one reason: to win the 1964 Daytona 500, which it did three more times. To produce the Street Hemi version, which debuted as a Plymouth Belvedere option in 1966, compression was dropped from 12.5 to 10.5:1, cast-iron exhaust headers replaced the tubular steel long-tube headers, and a new cast-iron intake manifold replaced the race engine's aluminum manifold. In addition, it used a new camshaft with less aggressive and more street-friendly valve timing, even though it used solid valve lifters (tappets) as the Race Hemi did.

Central to the Hemi's massive power output was the combustion chamber design inside the cylinder heads. The chamber itself was hemispherical (rounded) with the spark plug located at the top of the circle and the massive intake and exhaust valves located directly across the combustion chamber from each other. As Plymouth's *1970 Dealer Data Book* said, "This permits big, powerful fuel-air charges to enter from the intake port, deliver tremendous power to the piston, and exhaust directly across the chamber with minimum loss of flowing momentum. At high speeds, the Hemi breathes with ease, where ordinary engines have their power choked off."

In other words, it breathed in and out like a professional athlete in top physical condition. It was also just the thing for engines in Road Runners and other Plymouths to dominate the Super Stock and Pro Stock

There's no mistaking the engine under the hood. If the air cleaner does not tip you off, the valvecovers will. For 1970, only 75 hardtops, 74 coupes, and 3 convertible Road Runners received the legendary Hemi big-block engine.

classes at the drag strips. It also made "just running down the road" an intense physical thrill, once the "long pedal" was pressed to the floorboard and the two big Holley 4-barrel carburetors opened up.

For 1970, the major change to the 426 Hemi was an all-new hydraulic-lifter camshaft. Now, owners of street-driven Hemi-powered Road Runners did not have to remove the valvecovers and adjust the solid valve lifters to maintain peak engine performance. The new factory cam had the same .490-inch lift and 284-degree duration (intake and exhaust) specifications as the previous 1966–1969 solid-lifter Street Hemi camshaft. There was no drop-off in the Hemi's horsepower and torque with it; 425 hp and 490 ft-lbs of torque were still the peaks, although more than a few trackside observers believed those factory numbers were on the low side.

Other Hemi standard features for 1970 were carried over from 1969 and earlier. They included 10.2:1 compression; a dual-breaker distributor and "cold" heat-range spark plugs (differing from non-performance "hot" plugs by their short insulator tip and a design that removed heat from the combustion chamber quicker) for plenty of spark at high RPM; a wider (3/8-inch-diameter) fuel line than used on other Chrysler V-8 engines, to keep this beast of an engine well-fed; an oil pan windage tray, to minimize power loss from oil splashing on the crankshaft and causing drag; a double-roller timing chain; a seven-blade torque-driven fan with a fan shroud located behind a heavy-duty 26-inch-wide radiator that combined to keep the big engine cool; a skid plate under the oil pan to protect it from "wheelie"-induced damage on the strip (or steep driveways on the street); and appearance items such as black "crinkle finish" valvecovers and a chrome oil-filler cap.

Still standard with the 426 Hemi was its cylinder block's 4.89-inch cylinder bore spacing and 10.72-inch deck height, making it a massive engine; its four-bolt (and cross-bolt) main bearing caps, which few other engines offered as standard equipment; and a unique front crossmember (K-member) under it, specifically

The 426 Hemi graces the engine bay of this striking red hardtop. In 1970, Chrysler installed a hydraulic cam rather than the solid-lifter cam that required more frequent valvetrain adjustment. Similar to 426 Hemis from earlier years, this version featured 10.25:1 compression ratio, cast-iron exhaust manifolds, and twin Carter AFBs were perched on a dual-plane aluminum intake. (Photo Courtesy David Newhardt)

designed and engineered to hold the Hemi in place.

When you ordered a 426 Hemi in your 1970 Road Runner (for $841.05 over the base 383), you also received a 70-ampere-hour battery, the N96 Air Grabber cold-air induction system, F70-14 whitewall fiberglass-belted tires, and a heavy-duty A727 transmission; and the Hemi suspension system.

One thing you didn't receive with the Hemi was the standard Chrysler five-year/50,000-mile limited powertrain warranty, a Plymouth mainstay since 1963. Instead, Hemis were sold with an extremely limited 12-month/12,000-mile warranty that was available to the original purchaser only. That meant that if you saw one for sale as a used car before it was a year old, no factory warranty coverage was available on the engine at all,

and any parts breakage became the new owner's responsibility to repair.

What you did get with the 426 Hemi in 1970 was a race-engineered powerplant that, when properly tuned, was all but unbeatable, except by the 440 Six Barrel, which proved to be a more-street-friendly engine than the Hemi in factory-stock form.

The 1970 426 Street Hemi sat on a special front crossmember (the K-member) that was specially designed and engineered for the Hemi. 426 Hemis with engine mounts that bolted to the B/RB engine crossmember did not appear until 1993, when Mopar Performance released its reproduction 426 Hemi crate engine and cylinder block.

TRANSMISSIONS

If you ask Mopar devotees what the biggest change in manual transmissions was for the Road Runner for 1970, they point to the all-new, Hurst-sourced Pistol Grip shifter atop the A-833 4-speed. They are correct in terms of visual appearance and shifting function, but they are wrong on the big unseen gearbox change for 1970.

That was because that change made the A-833 4-speed an extra-cost option ($197.25) and made a heavy-duty floor-shifted 3-speed manual transmission standard. Like its larger counterpart, the 3-speed was fully synchronized in all forward gears. A new refinement to all Chrysler 3-speeds for 1970, and not just the version standard in the Road Runner, the newly-synchronized first gear did away with low-speed grinding and crunching noises that were sometimes

Seen here behind a Road Runner 383 is the A-833 4-speed manual transmission, likely the version with a 23-spline input shaft that all 383/4-speed cars received. Also visible at the top left is the starter motor; its gear-reduction construction (pioneered by Chrysler and now an industry standard) gave it a unique sound that Mopar lovers dubbed the "Highland Park Hummingbird." (Photo Courtesy Vanguard Motor Sales)

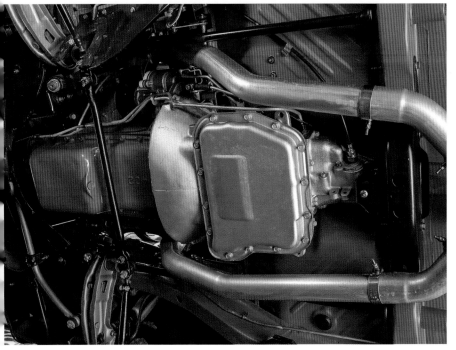

If you ordered a TorqueFlite automatic transmission without the center console option (Code C16), the gear selector was located on the steering column (shown). Unlike those on police-model Plymouths, which could not be shifted manually into first or second gears, the backward/forward switch on this Road Runner can be manually shifted through its three forward gears. Racers usually installed an aftermarket shifter or simply left it in Drive and kept both hands on the steering wheel. (Photo Courtesy Vanguard Motor Sales)

Here's Chrysler's 8¾-inch rear end, standard with 383-powered Road Runners. Note that there is no removable rear cover. Any servicing or repairs mean the axles and driveshaft must be removed first. (Photo Courtesy Vanguard Motor Sales)

heard when downshifting into first at low speeds.

The standard-transmission change also gave Chrysler-Plymouth dealers a price leader in the Road Runner line. When equipped with just a few options such as the AM radio (Code R11) or Rallye Road Wheels (Code R21), it could be advertised in newspaper ads for well under $3,000 (including tax, title, license fees, etc.).

With the 3-speed now the standard gearbox, the Road Runner's available transmissions were now the tried-and-true A-727 TorqueFlite automatic and the A-833 4-speed manual. Chrysler's 4-speed, built at its New Process Gear Division plant in DeWitt, New York, was available again in standard and Hemi (ultra-high-performance) versions, the latter with a stout 18-spline input shaft and other severe-service internal parts.

Both 4-speeds now wore the new Pistol Grip handles as part of their Hurst-supplied shifters. The Road Runner, as well as the GTX and Dodge's Coronet Super Bee, Coronet R/T, and Charger lineup, used a Pistol Grip shifter handle that was longer (and shaped to clear the Road Runner's standard front bench seat) than the

The Dana 60 rear axle was the top rear differential option and this rugged unit effectively transmitted the enormous torque of the 440 6-Pack and 426 Hemi. (Photo Courtesy Vanguard Motor Sales)

one used in the E-Body Barracuda and the A-Body Duster 340.

REAR-AXLE ASSEMBLIES AND DIFFERENTIALS

The power from the 383, 440 Six Barrel, and Hemi was effectively transferred to the road with option packages that combined either a Chrysler-made 8¾-inch rear end or the ultra-strong Dana 60 rear-axle assembly, Chrysler's Sure Grip limited-slip differential, and other performance-related features. These items included the "Hemi" suspension with special rear leaf springs, heavy-duty cooling, power brakes, and a dual-breaker distributor.

Standard wheel treatment, optional (In Violet) color. Base wheel trim for Road Runner in 1970 was once again a body-color-painted stamped steel wheel, wearing the plain Plymouth hub cap. However, radial-ply tires, let alone blackwalls, were not available on the Road Runner at the start of the 1970 model year; white sidewall F70-14 bias-ply tires were standard. The trailing edge of the rear quarter panel aft of wheel opening was a location prone to rust on cars driven where roads were de-iced with salt in the winter, and a location where prospective buyers of used 1970 Road Runners should look for rust damage or plastic filler used to try and repair it.

Road Runners with TorqueFlites behind their Hemis or 440 Six Barrels could be outfitted with the Code A32 Super Performance Axle Package. This put a 4.10 rear gear set inside a Sure Grip Dana 60. It also added the "Hemi" heavy-duty suspension, heavy-duty cooling, and power brakes.

The Hemi suspension used the existing Chrysler rear leaf-spring design and added thicker leaves to the spring bundles on each side and two special "half leaves" to the passenger-side spring bundle to better handle the flood of torque coming from the engine, while keeping the rear axle assembly properly located underneath the car. With it, no aftermarket parts, such as traction bars, were needed.

Shock absorbers were heavy-duty in the back, where they combined with the special leaf springs to keep the rear axle assembly properly located. They helped the fairly heavy (approaching 3,800 pounds) car handle around corners as well.

For those who wanted to grab gears (and make full use of that Hurst-shifted 18-spline A-833 4-speed), two performance-axle options were available, differentiated by the Dana 60 rears used in each one. The Code A33

Track Pak used a 3.54:1 ring-and-pinion gear; the Code A34 Super Track Pak featured a 4.10:1 gear set. Both Paks also included a heavy-duty Sure Grip differential, the "Hemi" suspension with an extra leaf on the right side to aid traction on hard launches (such as on a drag-strip), heavy-duty cooling that included a 26-inch-deep radiator, dual-breaker distributor, and power front disc/rear drum brakes.

Next was the Code A36 Performance Axle Package. Again, it was centered on the 8¾-inch rear-axle assembly that added $102.15 to a 383-powered Road Runner's sticker price. Although it was not available with the 3-speed stick or the Code A35 Trailer Towing Package, the Code A36 package was offered for $92.25 with 440 Six/TorqueFlite Birds and $64.80 with automatic-equipped Hemi cars.

For Road Runners with the two strongest engines (the Hemi and 440 Six), the Track Pak axle options included the Dana 60 rear end that was up to those engines' power. The Code A33 Track Pak, with its 3.54-geared Dana 60, cost $142.85 extra; the 4.10-geared Code A34 Super Track Pak added $235.65 to 4-speed Hemi and 440 Six Barrel Road Runners' stickers.

CHAPTER 3

BODY, CHASSIS AND SUSPENSION

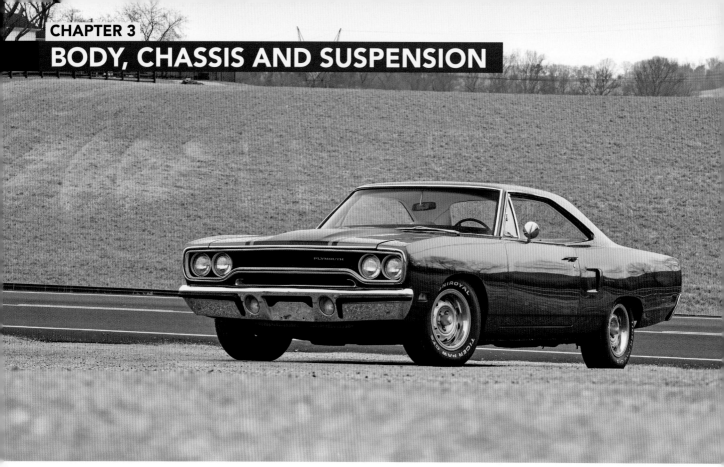

The 1970 Road Runner featured aggressive, updated exterior styling and the best high-performance drivetrain packages Plymouth offered, all built with Chrysler's rugged and reliable Unibody construction. For 1970, Road Runner was offered in three body styles: hardtop (shown), coupe, and convertible.

The 1970 model's new sheet metal and trim graced a substructure that had proven itself over the previous decade, with steering and suspension systems that benefited from ongoing development.

UNIBODY: SURROUNDING YOU WITH STRENGTH

Unlike competitive models, which relied on a separate body-on frame construction method, Chrysler's Unibody construction method "surrounded you with strength," as the company literature that touted their engineering advances proclaimed.

As the *1970 Plymouth Dealer Data Book* detailed it, "Unibody construction is tight and strong because all structural steel members, body braces, and sheet-metal panels are welded into a single, unitized shell in which all parts contribute to its overall strength. Steel sections used for roof side rails, body-side sills, floor supports, and door pillars are box-section members of heavy-gauge steel to ensure maximum strength and support."

Those components received a thorough "shaking out" even before the first prototype parts were fabricated and welded together, thanks to Chrysler's use of advanced information technology of the day, which had its roots in military/national defense work from the 1940s onward.

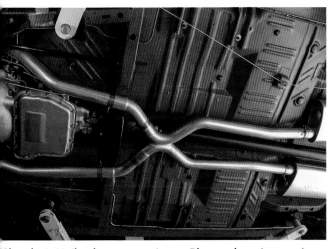

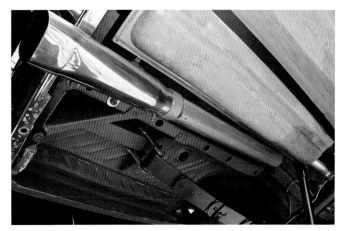

Chrysler's Unibody construction, a Plymouth mainstay since 1960, featured front and rear frame components welded directly to the floorpan, resulting in greater strength and lighter weight than body-on-frame construction offered. For additional strength, racers welded in subframe connectors (available via the aftermarket, or ones they fabricated themselves) that tied together the crossmember behind the transmission (at the left-center of photo) with the rear frame rails that flank the mufflers and the crossmember that the rear leaf springs bolt on to. (Photo Courtesy Vanguard Motor Sales)

Specifically, body designs were turned into three-dimensional renderings on an IBM 360 mainframe computer housed in the Engineering Department at Highland Park. The renderings were used to design 3/8-scale replicas of each Unibody component, which were then made out of clear plastic. The replica Unibody components were joined by simulated spot welds to form a model that could be used by body engineers

Here you see the rear leaf spring as well as the rear under-floor Unibody structural members, including the rear frame rail. Standard Road Runner shock absorbers were the heavy-duty descendants of the Oriflow shock absorber that Chrysler introduced during the 1950s to help give the cars "the boulevard ride." (Photo Courtesy Vanguard Motor Sales)

The driver-side rear frame rail (next to the chrome-tipped tailpipe) is a key member of the Unibody structure, along with its twin on the passenger's side. The inside of the driver-side rear quarter panel is an area susceptible to rust resulting from road salt, snow, and dirt. (Photo Courtesy Vanguard Motor Sales)

The strength of the B-Body platform that the Road Runner was built on comes from its design and construction, which added rigidity and strength while eliminating excess weight (such as a separate frame). The subframe rails have several support elements that tie into the chassis and inner fenderwell, which provides extra support and rigidity, especially under hard acceleration.

The rear subframe, suspension, and Dana 60 rear end readily handled the power from the 383 and 440 Six Barrel engines, as well as the 426 Hemi. (Photo courtesy Vanguard Motor Sales)

in the stress laboratory at Highland Park to locate high-stress points. Modifications or reinforcements were added to the replica body, making it less resistant to extreme bending and twisting. In turn, those modifications were added to the corresponding full-scale steel parts, long before the first tooling die to produce them was created.

Although the rear quarter panels were welded to the body, they were not load-bearing members providing structural strength to the car. That was unlike Hudson's experience with unit-body construction in the 1948–1954 "Step-Down" cars, which (although revolutionary for the late 1940s) proved to be nearly impossible to affordably update in styling. Hudson, as a low-volume manufacturer that could turn out no more than 100,000 to 150,000 cars per year, was stuck with a body design that became non-competitive in the new-car market of the early 1950s, especially after Chrysler, Ford, and General Motors rolled out their second-generation of post World War I cars beginning in 1952. (Hudson became part of American Motors (AMC) through a 1954 merger with Nash-Kelvinator. Chrysler acquired AMC in 1987.)

Specific structural components for all body styles, including convertibles, carried a rugged all-welded steel front structure forward of the windshield and firewall, box-section windshield pillars (A-pillars) and windshield headers, diagonal body braces, galvanized rocker panels (for extra corrosion protection), and heavy-gauge floor reinforcements.

Hardtop models also received structural reinforcements in their rear roof pillars (C-pillars) and roof support bows, Coupes also received box-section door pillars (B-pillars), and all 426 Hemi-powered cars received the same "torque box" reinforcements in front of the rear leaf spring hangers that convertible bodies received, along with a welded-in reinforcement plate located directly over the rear axle assembly's pinion snubber. That last reinforcement removed a source of rear floorpan caving resulting from high-RPM launches.

Although they were in their final year of production in 1970, B-Body convertible Unibodies also received flat-steel reinforcements that reached across the body front cross-member to the body-side seams.

Once welded together, the "body in white," so called because of its "white metal" (unpainted) state, was then bonderized (phosphate coated) before a series of six chemical sprays, followed by seven dips into chemical baths and electrostatically-charged primer, coated the entire body assembly. That included boxed-in areas inside the body where coatings that were merely sprayed onto a passing body could never reach.

After that, the body then received two coats of acrylic enamel paint, which were baked to a hard finish in huge ovens through which the body shop's line rolled.

Once inspectors approved it, the painted Unibody was trimmed inside and out, and made ready for the "body drop" on the final assembly line, where it joined the powertrain, suspension, and steering parts that awaited it on a special jig at the head of the final line.

The anti-corrosion process was the result of the negative experience with Chrysler Corporation's entire 1957 passenger car lineup. The bodies of those low-slung high-finned "Forward Look" cars (not just from Plymouth, but also from Dodge, De Soto, Chrysler, and Imperial) started showing rust perforation within a year. Body engineers and plant engineers alike later said that those all-new bodies were at least six months away from being ready for production but were rushed into production to meet the deadline set by Chrysler's upper management. Once the corrosion problems surfaced, sales across the board dropped.

Standard Road Runner shock absorbers were the heavy-duty descendants of the Oriflow unit. Chrysler introduced them during the 1950s to give its cars "the boulevard ride." Visible here are the rear leaf spring and the rear underfloor Unibody structural members, including the rear frame rails. (Photo Courtesy Vanguard Motor Sales)

That was a key factor in the De Soto brand's demise within the next five years.

Quick fixes solved some body-quality problems in the later 1957s, as well as in 1958 and 1959 models (such as excessive water leakage in rainy weather), but major structural-quality improvements were achieved when Chrysler converted its high-volume production to the Unibody for 1960. (All but Imperial, which remained body-on-frame through 1966 with the same seven-step dip and spray anti-corrosion process added.)

SUSPENSION: "TORSION-AIRE" FOR THE BIRD

All Chrysler passenger cars in 1970 used the Torsion-Aire suspension system when it was introduced for 1957.

Key to it were longitudinal torsion bars and control arms in front and asymmetrical leaf spring bundles in the rear, along with Chrysler's own Oriflow shock absorbers at each corner.

The front suspension kept the Road Runner going where you pointed it. The torsion bar suspension features upper and lower control arms. As you can see the anti-sway bar attaches to the lower control arm, which is next to the front torsion bar. (Courtesy Vanguard Motor Sales)

The high-chromium-content steel front torsion bars were lighter than conventional coil springs and used a twisting motion instead of the coil springs' compress/release cycles. That led to "superior ride and handling control [with] safe, responsive handling in turns on superhighways and over rough roads," per the 1970 *Plymouth Dealer Data Book*.

The Road Runner's front torsion bars, which it shared with GTX and police- and taxi-package Belvederes, had a larger diameter (.90 inch) than the versions used on standard Belvedere, Satellite, and Sport Satellite models (.88 inch). Hemi and 440 Six Barrel Birds received even thicker torsion bars, a hefty .92 inch in diameter.

Regardless of engine size, a .94-inch-diameter front anti-sway bar was standard equipment, all the better to help the Bird corner in the same manner as it accelerated and braked: briskly. In the rear, Chrysler used leaf springs on the Road Runner (as Ford did on its midsize Torino and Mercury Montego models in 1970), which

were asymmetrically mounted, with the rear-axle assembly mounted forward of the springs' fore/aft midpoint. Combined with angled front-wheel control arms, they helped the car resist front-end dive under heavy braking and rear-end squat under acceleration. The 426 Hemi and 440 Six Barrel cars had two half-leaves (actually, two short leaves) in its passenger-side rear spring bundles, to help keep the rear end, axle assembly, and tires in place under hard acceleration. At each corner, tubular shock absorbers were used to limit wheel travel.

STEERING

Recirculating-ball steering gears were common across the U.S. auto industry at the start of the 1970s; the modern lightweight rack-and-pinion systems were not yet in production. Standard steering on 1970 Road Runners was a manual, non-power-assisted recirculating-ball system with a 24:1 gear ratio (28.8:1 overall ratio), which took 5.3 turns of the steering wheel to move the front wheels from full-left to full-right, assisted only by the driver's upper-body strength. These manual steering boxes were dubbed "Armstrong steering" by auto enthusiasts. I met some retired California Highway Patrol (CHP) officers who drove Chrysler-built, manual-steering-equipped patrol cars while on duty; their handshake nearly flattened my right hand and pulled my right arm off at the shoulder, thanks to their years of driving cars so equipped!

Power steering (Code S77) was optional, which added a hydraulic pump driven by a belt off the engine to its 15.7:1 gear ratio (18.8:1 overall ratio) to reduce steering effort to just 3.5 turns of the steering wheel from full left to full right. With either power or manual steering, the 1970 Road Runner's turning diameter was slightly more than 40 feet.

The Road Runner's steering boxes, manual and power, were shared with Belvedere police models, whose advertising in 1968 included the line, "Why Plymouth? Take a 20 mph corner in one. At 60."

BRAKES

One word describes the standard Road Runner drum-and-shoe brakes: big. At 11 inches in diameter, they were the largest size used on any Chrysler passenger car. They benefited from years of research on advanced high-temperature materials (one of my father's areas of research in Chrysler's materials lab from 1953 to 1959). That resulted in improved brake linings, which Chrysler's Total Contact brakes of the 1950s pioneered. These had linings bonded to the brake shoe instead of riveted, which left holes on the brake lining that led to uneven brake wear.

The drum's 11-inch diameter, combined with the Total Contact linings, gave braking performance that was superior to other cars' brakes that used riveted linings and drums as small as 9 inches in diameter.

Moreover, as these brakes had been included with the heavy-duty 361, 383, and 426 wedge-engine packages from 1962 onward on both civilian and police-model B-Body Plymouths, they were the most highly advanced drum-and-shoe brake system Chrysler offered. Power assist (Code B51) was available, if you didn't mind the extra weight the booster added or the $42.95 option price subtracted from your wallet.

The front torsion bars are visible just to the outside of this Road Runner's exhaust pipes, connected to the lower control arms on each side. The front anti-sway bar is located forward of the oil pan's sump and routed through the engine K-member, as well as the optional front disc brakes. (Photo Courtesy Vanguard Motor Sales)

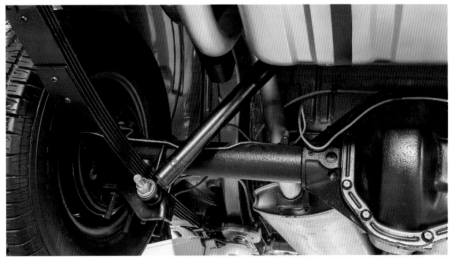

The Road Runner's available Hemi rear suspension features a passenger-side rear leaf-spring bundle, with the "half leaves" visible at the bottom of the spring bundle, all to keep the rear of the car firmly planted on the ground once the 426 Hemi loads the Unibody with its 490 ft-lbs of torque. Also note the rear drum brake; factory-installed rear disc brakes were still far in the future in 1970. (Photo Courtesy Vanguard Motor Sales)

By 1970, Chrysler was on its second disc-brake design; a single-piston caliper design replaced a more-complicated four-piston design that was used in full-size cars starting in 1965. Disc brakes have one big advantage over drums: the rotor and pads are exposed to the air and can cool more rapidly than drums, which helps prevent brake fading during severe use. (Photo Courtesy Vanguard Motor Sales)

However, they were still drum brakes, whose inherent flaws included a tendency to overheat (to the extent that brake performance decreased dramatically) in repeated hard-braking conditions. In rainy or otherwise wet conditions, water adversely affected drum/brake lining effectiveness. Either way, a sudden loss of brakes was a serious possibility.

Disc brakes used calipers with pads made of the same materials as drum brake linings to grab a rotor that was bolted to the wheel. That solved the problems of heat and moisture leading to brake failure and reduced unsprung weight (weight not supported by the car's suspension) as well.

Disc brakes made their first appearance on full-size Chryslers, Dodges, Imperials, and Plymouths in 1966 with a four-piston disc-brake system sourced from Bendix. By 1970, Chrysler had changed to a single-piston

disc sourced from Kelsey-Hayes; this was used on the Road Runner in 1970.

Although Chrysler was researching four-wheel disc-brake systems by then, with an early anti-lock brake system (ABS) in the works for the Imperial, those braking advances were not yet available for any Chrysler vehicle in 1970.

Rear disc brakes were not offered on the Road Runner for 1970. Cost considerations, namely competition against low-price rivals Chevrolet, Ford, and AMC (which didn't offer them on any of their steel-bodied, midsize cars that year), and the fact that the standard rear drums worked well in tandem with the available front discs without adding brake-system parts such as front/rear proportioning valves, led to the front disc/rear drum option.

If you wanted that optional braking system on your 1970 Road Runner, it meant ordering Code B41 for the front disc brakes ($27.90) along with Code B51 for the rear power brakes ($42.95),bringing the total extra cost of power front disc/rear drums to $70.85.

WHEELS

At the Bird's corners, wheel and tire choices started with the standard body-color 14 x 6–inch steel wheel with plain hubcap. It then proceeded through a choice of 14- and 15-inch wheels that included the five-spoke wheel option available on the Road Runner since 1968, as well as an all-new steel road wheel option that was shown prominently on Road Runners in Plymouth ads and dealer literature.

New steel Rallye road wheels (Code W21) replaced the cast-aluminum wheel option that appeared in the 1969 sales brochures and dealer literature but were recalled just days before the 1969 cars went on sale. A design flaw prevented the lug nuts from being tightened to the specified torque, and if anyone tried to force the lug nuts on by over-torquing them, the wheels cracked.

As for tires, wide tread was the key. The standard tire size was F70-14, in your choice of standard whitewall or optional raised-white-letter versions, with ultra-wide (for 1970) F60-15 raised-white-letter tires optional. F70-14 blackwalls were not offered on the Road Runner.

Available only in a 14-inch diameter in 1970, the chrome five-spoke wheel option was popular then and remains popular today, as its reproduction by the aftermarket attests.

The Code W21 Rallye Road Wheel option became available for 1970 in 14 x 6– and 15 x 7–inch sizes. These steel wheels replaced the trouble-prone cast-aluminum "recall" wheels from 1969. However, they never appeared on a car released for sale because of problems with the wheels' centers. These wheels are available through the aftermarket in stock sizes and 17-inch diameters. (Photo Courtesy Vanguard Motor Sales)

I don't know if this tire is the original spare installed in the trunk on the assembly line in 1970 or a later reproduction, but this gives you an idea of what the F70-14 tires looked like. Standard tires had white sidewalls; Aries white-letter tires like these were optional. (Photo Courtesy Vanguard Motor Sales)

CHAPTER 4

INTERIOR, EXTERIOR AND PACKAGES

A Hemi Road Runner is one rare bird. For 1970, 75 of them were built as hardtops, and only 16 carried the 727 TorqueFlite automatic. This example is equipped with the A32 Super Performance Axle Package with 4.10 gears for staggering acceleration between stoplights. (Photo Courtesy David Newhardt)

For many new-car buyers, regardless of brand or model, the vehicle's looks (in person and in perception) was one of the most important selling points. That not only included a car's styling, but also the colors and trims that graced it inside and out.

The Chrysler Corporation product planners also had another consideration for the Plymouth lineup and the colors its 1970 models would wear: how to increase curb appeal at a time when bright, vibrant colors appeared often in daily life. That challenge was magnified in a way by the "budget muscle car" nature of the Road Runner, which had become known and popular for offering spartan interior trim and a minimum of exterior ornamenta-tion. If potential buyers wanted fancier trim and more brightwork than the Road Runner offered, GTX had the added "plushness" (by 1970 low-price car standards, at least) they were looking for.

Plymouth's product planners could have taken the easy route when it was time to specify the 1970 Road Runner's interior and exterior style elements, both standard and optional. They could have chosen to carry over the 1969 color and trim choices, a sensi-ble cost-controlling move considering that an all-new B-Body was coming for 1971. New colors, seat designs, etc., could wait until then. One example was the optional front bucket seats, a tried-and-true low-back choice that had accepted federally mandated head restraints for 1969 without looking tacked on. Cost considerations could have kept them on the Road Runner options list for another year, along with the dashboard design and interior upholstery selections, as well as exterior paint, stripe, and vinyl-top choices.

Other bucket-seat choices for 1970 included this black/charcoal-gray style, one of nine bucket-seat color choices available that year. The front floor mat is an aftermarket accessory. (Photo Courtesy Vanguard Motor Sales)

Optional bucket seats and a center console dress up this 1970 Road Runner coupe. The taper of the seatbacks allowed the occupant to turn around more easily and see behind than other high-back bucket-seat designs from Ford, General Motors, and AMC. (Photo Courtesy Vanguard Motor Sales)

The last year that the Road Runner coupe models featured flip-out rear quarter windows was 1970. The rear-window up/down mechanism was eliminated in the name of weight and cost savings. The 1970 models also had a cloth headliner, which Chrysler replaced during that decade with molded-plastic versions. (Photo Courtesy Vanguard Motor Sales)

The standard bench seats were available in eight colors, including white (shown). Front headrests, required by federal motor-vehicle safety standards that year, remained the same as those used on 1969 bench and bucket seats. The center console is an aftermarket item.

At the top of the line when it came to interior trims was the bucket seat option, which was available with the Code C16 center console (shown) or the available C21 folding armrest and "buddy seat." Leather seating surfaces weren't offered on the Road Runner for 1970; among Plymouths, they were a GTX exclusive that year, in Plymouth's "upscale" muscle car.

The Road Runner shared its new 1970 instrument panel, which featured the optional 8,000-rpm tachometer, with the Dodge Charger. Note the various switch locations on the dash, the console-mounted automatic shifter, and the placement of the cartoon bird's smiling face in the middle of the available deluxe steering wheel. (Photo Courtesy David Newhardt)

Instead, they added noticeable changes for the last-year Bird before the scheduled 1971 redesign. The optional front bucket seats received a stylish, yet functional upgrade (as did the interior upholstery choices); the Rallye gauge cluster from the Dodge Charger's dashboard was now a Road Runner standard feature, and the Bird's plumage became more vivid for 1970.

INTERIOR OPTIONS

Inside, 1970 meant a continuation of interior comfort and convenience options that Plymouth had offered since the Road Runner's inception. The coupe's standard bench-seat interior still wore a plain all-vinyl trim shared with the base Belvedere coupe, but the hardtop and convertible standard front and rear bench seats wore

Another item that was first available in 1970, and became an instant classic among Mopar lovers: the Hurst Pistol Grip shifter for the optional 4-speed manual transmission. Seen here is the long-handle version that was used on the Road Runner, as well as on the other 4-speed Plymouth and Dodge B-Body cars, whose handle cleared the standard front bench seat. The reverse-gear indicator light is on the dash just to the right of the shifter, the dash wears an optional Code R11 AM radio, and the ignition switch is on the steering column, an anti-theft feature introduced across the board in all U.S.-built Chrysler Corporation passenger cars in 1970. (Courtesy Mecum Auctions)

an upgraded all-vinyl upholstery shared with the Satellite, which was included with the Road Runner Decor Package on the coupe. Front bucket/rear bench seats were available for $100.85 extra, and a center ("buddy") seat cushion with a fold-down armrest cost $54.45 extra (Code C21) but only on Birds with column-mounted TorqueFlite automatic transmissions.

If you wanted a center console instead, especially if you had a 4-speed manual gearbox or wanted the TorqueFlite's gear lever mounted on the floor, you checked the box for Code C16 on the order blank and added $54.45 to the sticker price. In addition, if you wanted the extra convenience of six-way (fore/aft and up/down) adjustment to your driver-side bucket seat, the C62 Comfort Position six-way manual seat adjuster added that convenience for just $30.90 extra.

As previously mentioned, the Road Runner's dash cluster was restyled for 1970 with a round, 150-mph speedometer now standard. A 7,000-rpm tachometer combined with an analog clock (nicknamed the "Tick-Tock Tach") was Code N85 on the options list and $68.45 extra.

For factory-installed sound systems, you had four

The optional C16 center console contained a shifter for the Code D34 TorqueFlite automatic transmission or the Code D21 Pistol Grip 4-speed, and added a big storage bin between the seats for just $54.45 extra. The final year that this particular TorqueFlite shifter was used on the Road Runner was 1970; for 1971, it was succeeded by the Slap Stick console-mounted shifter that was first used on the E-Body 1970 Plymouth Barracuda and Dodge Challenger. (Courtesy Mecum Auctions)

How blue can you get? In the case of the optional P6B5 blue all-vinyl front bucket/rear seat trim that this 1970 Road Runner hardtop wears (along with its EB5 Blue Fire Metallic paint) was the only blue one offered among the nine colors and/or color combinations. It was 1970 that marked the first year for high-back bucket seats, the steering column-mounted ignition switch, and the Hurst Pistol Grip 4-speed shifter. Front-door vent windows made their final B-Body appearance for 1970.

The (R22) AM radio with tape player was optional for the 1970 Road Runner. The base was a standard AM radio (R11). A solid state AM/FM radio (R21) was another option.

The 150-mph speedometer features an attractive chrome bezel and is sensibly positioned in this standard dash. The fuel gauge is also conveniently positioned next to the speedometer.

choices. The solid-state push-button AM radio (Code R11) that was included with the Code A04 Basic Group cost an additional $61.55, the solid-state push-button AM/FM radio (Code R21) added $134.95, and the AM radio/stereo 8-track tape player (Code R22) added $196.25.

Coupe and hardtop models could have a rear speaker (Code R31) for $14.05 extra. If you ordered the Code A04 package, you could purchase the Code R35 AM/FM for a $73.50 upcharge, with the Code R37 AM/8-track available for $134.75 more.

What was the fourth factory sound system? No radio at all, saving the weight, albeit only about 5 to 7 pounds of the in-dash tuner and speaker. A plastic block-off plate, with the same camera-case surface texture as the rest of the dash, covered the radio opening stamped into the dash. That allowed the driver and passengers to enjoy their Bird's engine and exhaust sounds to their fullest, uninterrupted by AM radio static, FM radio-signal drift, obnoxious disc jockeys, irritating commercials played over and over and over, or the 8-track player mangling a tape because its playback head and pinch roller hadn't been cleaned in months.

Factory-installed air conditioning was available once

again on the Road Runner, via Chrysler's proven inte-grated heater, windshield defroster, and air conditioning system that was engineered and built by its Airtemp Division. However, it was only available on 383 Road Runners, and without the Air Grabber cold-air system (Code N96). Checking the box for Code H51 added the Airtemp system for $357.67 extra, the next-priciest factory option after the Hemi. If you ordered air condi-tioning, tinted glass was a recommended option, and Code G11 added it to all windows except the convert-ible's back window for $40.70 extra. Just the tinted windshield was Code G15 and cost $25.90 extra.

Many showroom customers and potential Road Runner buyers thought the new front bucket seats for 1970 made for one cool cabin. Incorporating a seat design that held its occupant in place, the front buckets were redesigned for 1970 to incorporate the headrest that federal safety standards had required since January 1, 1969. The seatback tapered inward near its top, making it easier for drivers to turn around and look back while reversing the car, something that Ford's and Mercury's newly redesigned high-back bucket seats didn't have.

You had a choice of nine colors for the 1970 Road

Although separate lap and shoulder belts were the rule for front-seat passengers in 1970, many eschewed the shoulder belt, wearing only the lap belt. Chrysler did not introduce three-point front lap/shoulder belts on any passenger car until 1973. (Photo Courtesy Vanguard Motor Sales)

Runner's all-vinyl bucket seats: Blue (Code P6B5), Green (Code P6F8), Burnt Orange (Code P6K4), Charcoal and Black (Code P6XA), Tan (Code P6T5), Gold and Black (Code P6XY), White and Black (Code P6XW), White and Burnt Orange (Code P6KW), and White and Blue (Code P6BW). Green and Tan were not available on convertibles, and the two-color interiors featured the first color on the seats, doors, and rear side panels, and the second color on the dash, steering column, carpets, and coupe/hardtop headliner.

For the standard hardtop and convertible models, as well as for coupes with the A87 Decor Group option, their all-vinyl split-front and rear bench seats were available in Blue (Code H2B5), Green (Code H2F8), Burnt Orange (Code H2K4), Black (Code H2X9), Tan (Code H2T5), White and Blue (Code H2BW), White and Burnt Orange (Code H2KW), and White and Black (Code H2XW). As with the bucket-seat trims, Green and Tan weren't available on convertibles, and the two-color trims' second color was on its carpets, dash, steering column, and hardtop/coupe headliners.

The base-level Road Runner coupe interior trims, shared with the base Belvedere, were available in Black (Code M2X9), Blue (Code

Only the finest faux woods were used on the optional Code S81 three-spoke steering wheel, another B-Body Plymouth option-list mainstay that returned for 1970, and cost $26.75 extra on hardtops and convertibles ($32.10 extra on the coupe). Also seen here is the column-mounted gear selector for the optional D34 TorqueFlite automatic transmission, the default location for this "go backward/go forward" switch unless the C16 console was also ordered. White-face gauges are a reverse-color aftermarket version of the standard gauges with black background and white markings.

Visual changes for the Road Runner, and all other 1969 midsize Plymouths, were minimal. Big, new taillights at each corner shed their built-in backup lights, and the 'Bird's trunk lid didn't have a Satellite or GTX metal trim insert as an option.

50

1970 Plymouth Road Runner
In Detail No. 10

M2B5), and Tan (Code M2T5).

For coupe and hardtop models, as well as for convertibles with the option for front shoulder belts (Code C13, which was $26.45 extra), 1970 also meant the return of the tangle of safety belts in front, as in 1968 and 1969, with separate lap and shoulder belts. (Three-point combined front lap/shoulder belts did not become standard in Chrysler Corporation passenger cars until 1973.) Standard belts were black, but color-keyed belts for front and rear were included with the option for deluxe seat belts (Code C15), which cost $13.75. If you wanted rear shoulder belts for your hardtop or coupe, Code C14 had the factory install them for $26.45 extra.

The standard Road Runner steering wheel (a plain, three-spoke version that was also standard on Belvedere models) was color-keyed to the interior, although more than a few racers replaced it with an aftermarket item made of a thicker foam rubber or vinyl rim. Savvy shoppers could replace it with a wood-grain three-spoke wheel (Code S81) that was carried over from 1969 and priced at $26.75 extra on hardtop and convertible models or $32.10 extra on coupes without the Code A87 Decor Package. (With Code A87, it was $26.75 extra.) In addition, the two-spoke, rim-blow wheel (Code S83) borrowed from the full-size C-Body Plymouth was

The rear view of the distinctive taillight panel shows this In Violet (Code FC7) Road Runner wearing a White (Code V8W) rear stripe along with a rear spoiler, which was a dealer-installed item was not listed in the *Salesman's Pocket Guide* as a Road Runner option at the start of the 1970 model year. (It was a Barracuda option, Code J81.) Also seen here is the one-year-only 1970 taillight assembly, which was considerably larger than those used on 1968 and 1969 Road Runners. (Photo Courtesy David Newhardt)

Vinyl tops, such as this 1970 Gator Grain Black option, were a stylish (and profitable) option in the late 1960s and early 1970s, giving a car a convertible-like appearance. However, over time these tops permitted water to seep through them, leading to corrosion problems on and along the roof panel (which wasn't painted on vinyl-topped cars). (Photo Courtesy Vanguard Motor Sales)

There's no mistaking the Road Runner for any other "budget muscle car," and no mistaking this In Violet example for anything but a 1970 version. (Photo Courtesy Vanguard Motor Sales)

a Road Runner option that added $19.15 to hardtop and convertible models and $29.00 to coupes that did not have the Code A87 option (or $16.05 with the Code A87 option).

OTHER OPTIONS

The rest of the Road Runner's factory options list was similar to its regular-performance Satellite, Sport Satellite, and Belvedere stablemates. A forced-air rear-window defogger (Code H31) was $26.25 extra on hardtops and coupes only. Code J55 purchased factory-applied undercoating and an underhood-mounted silencer pad for just $16.60 extra. In addition, the same array of body-side moldings and bumper guards that the Belvederes and

What goes into a dust trail? Not just dust, as this side detail shows. The stripe is actually made of reflective materia that shines gold when a light, such as a headlight, hits it at night. The trail "emerging" from the rear-quarter side scoops is a nod to animator Chuck Jones' tendency to have the cartoon Bird disappear into tunnels, etc., that Wile E. Coyote painted on the side of a mountain (and be surprised by a truck coming the other way when he went into that "tunnel" to chase the Bird!).

Satellites/Sport Satellites offered were Road Runner options as well. Door edge guards (Code M05) were $4.65 extra; belt-line molding (Code M31), standard on convertibles, was $21.15 extra on steel-topped Birds; custom sill molding (Code M25) was an extra $13.60; and rear bumper guards (Code M83) added some low-speed collision protection for $16.00 extra.

For those seeking to register their Birds in California, the Evaporative Emissions Control System (Code N95) was a required option, available with all engines, for an extra $37.85. (That was in addition to the different carburetors that California-bound Birds received, which helped those cars comply with California's clean-air standards.) The 383 and 440 Six Barrel Road Runners also required the Noise Reduction Package (Code N97) to make them legal in California. It was no extra charge, but it removed the chrome tips and low-restriction exhaust pipes from the standard dual-exhaust system and replaced them with quieter, standard-performance pipes with non-chrome, turned-down tips.

DRESSING THE BIRD

When it came to plumage for the Bird, 1970 was a most colorful year. Seven extra-cost ($14.05) High Impact colors were offered for 1970: In Violet (Code FC7), Tor Red (Code EV2), Lime Light (Code FJ5), Vitamin C Orange (Code EK2), and Lemon Twist (Code FY1). Two more joined them in February 1970: Sassy Grass Green (Code FJ6) and Moulin Rouge (Code FM3).

For those opting for the standard color selection, the choices included Black Velvet (Code TX9), Alpine White (Code EW1), Blue Fire Metallic (Code EB5), Jamaica Blue Metallic (Code EB7), Lime Green Metallic (Code FF4), Ivy Green Metallic (Code EF8), Deep Burnt Orange Metallic (Code FK5), Yellow Gold (Code DY3), Sandpebble Beige (Code BL1), Rally Red (Code FE5), Burnt Tan Metallic (Code FT6), Citron Mist Metallic (Code FY4), and Ice Blue Metallic (Code EB3). If you wanted one of the other 1970 Chrysler Corporation colors, such as those from the Imperial or Chrysler color palettes, they could be sprayed on at the factory, with a "999" code appearing on the fender tag line where the paint code went and a "Special Order Paint" notation on a second fender tag.

Available as a separate option, or with the Code A87 Decor Group on the coupe, this new transverse rear stripe sat across the trunk lid and adjoining quarter-panel corners, available in Black (Code V8X, shown), White (Code V8W), or Gold (Code V8Y). Again, note the "Seven Arts" under the cartoon Bird. By the time this appeared in production for 1970, the studio's name had been shortened to its original Warner Bros. In recent years, this stripe has been reproduced to replace worn or missing originals or to add an accent where a car may not have had one originally.

Road Runner buyers had three color choices when it came to the reflective tape stripe across the trunk lid and taillight panel for their A87-equipped coupe, hardtop, or convertible: Black (Code V8X), White (Code V8W), or Gold (Code V8Y). Along the sides was a new $15.55 tape-stripe option with a side view of a running road runner on the front fenders and a reflective Dust Trail stripe reaching back along the door and rear quarter panels before ending at the simulated side scoops. In front, a matte-black performance hood paint (Code V21) was an $18.05 option that blacked out the center of the hood where a center bulge hid the available Air Grabber hood scoop.

With vinyl tops increasing in popularity each year, not only with Plymouth, but also with every other U.S. carmaker, they were once again options on the Road Runner coupe and hardtop. The extra charge for the factory-installed textured roof treatment was $95.70, and it was available for 1970 in Black (Code V1X), White (Code V1W), Green (Code V1F), and Gator Grain Black (Code V1G). If you wanted a different-color vinyl top, it was yours with a factory-installed top and enough vinyl dye in your preferred color to get the job done.

But if you wanted one of the floral-pattern "Mod Tops" that had been available in 1968 and 1969, you were out of luck as far as a factory-installed version went. That option was only available on the Barracuda for 1970.

Convertible buyers also had a choice of top colors: Black (Code V3X) and White (Code V3W). As with the 1970 Fury and Satellite convertibles, but unlike Barracuda's drop tops, a power-operated convertible top was standard.

PACKAGES

New Road Runner interior items for 1970 included available high-back bucket seats with integral headrests, six new optional High Impact paint colors (for an extra $14.05), and an available Dust Trail reflective-tape stripe along each side. The stripe stretched from the leading edge of the front fender across the door and into the simulated scoop on each rear quarter panel; it looked like the cartoon bird was kicking up while running down the road (his idea of having fun). Those features joined the other new standard items shared with other B-Body Plymouths. These included standard front bumper guards; a column-mounted ignition switch with a key-in warning buzzer; column-mounted, four-way emergency flashers; lane-change turn signals; combination side-marker lights and reflectors; air-foam seat cushions; and a glove-box door that now hinged at the bottom and sported a rotary latch. Additional options included a rim-blow steering wheel and stainless-steel hood pins.

Those new and returning features added up to a budget muscle car that still had a model priced under $3,000. The base Road Runner coupe's sticker price started at $2,896, the hardtop's pricing started at $3,034, and the convertible's base sticker price was $3,289, proving once again that "if the top goes down, the price goes up." The manufacturer's suggested retail price included a 7-percent Federal Excise Tax and, per the 1970 *Plymouth Salesman's Pocket Guide*, "handling and other charges, and Factory Retail Provision For Dealer New-Car Preparation of $25.00."

The Road Runner and its Belvedere/Satellite/Sport Satellite/GTX brethren were offered with the widest range of options yet for Plymouth's midsize range, starting with option groups that combined multiple features and equipment into one easy-to-order package. The Code A01 Light Package added fender-mounted (or back-of-the-hood-bulge on the Road Runner) front turn signals, a trunk light, a glove-box light, a map/courtesy light, and a time-delay ignition light (none of which were available as separate options) to a new Road Runner, as well as $29.60 to its sticker price.

Ordering the Code A04 Basic Group added $177.20 to the sticker and included power steering, a remote-controlled driver-side exterior mirror, and a solid-state, push-button AM radio, although any other available radio could be included if you paid the difference between it and the AM tuner.

Base-level coupes could once again receive an upgrade from their Belvedere-level trimmings (such as they were) with the Code A87 Road Runner Decor Group. Similar to the interior and exterior decor packages available starting in mid-1968, this one included Satellite-grade, all-vinyl seat trim, a bright B-Pillar molding, a three-spoke steering wheel with partial horn ring and the cartoon bird's smiling face in the center button, door/side panel brightwork, and a rear transverse tape stripe, all for $81.50 extra. And, if you wanted to tow a trailer with your 383/TorqueFlite 'Bird, the Code A35 Trailer Towing Package upgraded its chassis and powertrain for that duty for just $14.05 more.

Pricing for optional performance-axle packages depended on the engine and transmission. Track Pak/Super Track Pak option groups were not available with Airtemp air conditioning. (Racers didn't want the added weight of the system, and Chrysler didn't want the headache of replacing air conditioning compressors under warranty that failed at high speed.)

Code A31 denoted the High Performance Axle Package available for 383-powered and non–air conditioning Birds. It included 3.91:1 gears. a Sure Grip limited-slip-differential 8¾-inch rear end, a 26-inch radiator with a seven-blade torque-drive fan, and Hemi suspension for an extra $102.15.

The 1970 Road Runner was not meant for mild touring, but rather all-out high-performance service. Tony D'Agostino's 383-powered Road Runner with Air Grabber hood, A-833 4-speed, and 8-3/4 rear differential is put through its paces just like magazine test cars back in the day. (Photo Courtesy Geoff Stunkard)

The Road Runner was in its third year and had few mechanical changes other than the full-year availability of the 440 Six Barrel engine option. However, the motoring press still put the 1970 Road Runner through its paces for its readers, especially with two all-new Plymouths with performance versions of their own: the all-new E-Body 'Cuda and the A-Body Duster 340.

Motor Trend magazine tested a 440 Six Barrel 4-speed Road Runner hardtop for a three-way road test in its December 1969 issue ("A Date With Three Strippers," written by A. B. Shuman). The test also included Chevrolet's new Chevelle SS454 with a pro-

totype 450-hp 454 that became the RPO LS6 engine option, as well as Ford's Torino Cobra fastback with the new-for-1970 429 Cobra Jet engine.

The options on each test car took them out of "budget muscle car" range, as Shuman pointed out in his mention of the Road Runner. "The window sticker on our hardtop started at $3,034 and totaled out at $4,417 delivered," wrote Shuman, as he noted the test car's factory-installed powerplant. "The engine is rated at 390 hp at 4,700 rpm and carries three Holley 2-barrel carbs. These carburetors were designed specifically for this setup and shouldn't be confused with the new Holley

A factory-built dragstrip-ready engine that could run with the Hemis, yet cost far less on the sticker than the Elephant engine? That's the 440 Six Barrel, which *Super Stock & Drag Illustrated* drove into the mid-13s on the strip, with some tuning help. (Photo Courtesy David Newhardt)

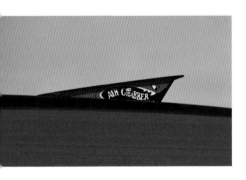

Open wide, inhale mass quantities of cool outside air, and watch the elapsed times drop. Keeping the Air Grabber open not only helped the big engines' performance on the strip, but they were also an intimidating factor while the Bird was staging next to its opponent. (Photo Courtesy David Newhardt)

a smoother application of power and works better than a mechanical linkage.

"The Road Runner's particular brand of fresh-air delivery system is the Air Grabber, which is timed to come up within the interval of a stop light; it's illuminated with the same eyes and teeth that distinguished the Flying Tigers' P-40s back in World War II. When not in use, it lies flush with the top of the domed hood, away from prying eyes and fingers."

So, how did it perform? Admirably, per Shuman, even though there were problems at the track and with the track. "On the day we took the car to Irwindale Raceway, the wind had blown a light coating of sand onto the track surface. Even with those 8½-inch-wide Polyglas GTs, it was possible to take off from an idle and spin the tires all the way through first and most of second gear."

Still, the 440 Six Barrel hardtop posted strong times despite the sand on the track and a shifter that was hard to shift under power, which, Shuman noted, was probably due to the car not being fully "run in" before they took it to the

500-cfm 2-barrel. Actually, their combined airflow capacity is about 1,100 cfm, with the center carburetor being smaller than the outboard two.

"Idling and common cruising is handled by the center jug, simplifying the emissions situation, with the auxiliary carburetors coming in 'when needed,' determined by engine vacuum. Vacuum actuation results in

track. "Despite the traction and shifting problems, the Tor Red Road Runner ran consistent mid-14-second quarters, with a best of 14.4 and a worst of 15.1. The speeds ranged between 94 and 99 mph.

"The car did have the best passing speeds, taking only 2.8 seconds to go from 40 to 60 mph and 3.2 to make it from 50 to 70, both in third gear. (For

There was no stronger rear-axle assembly under any American muscle car than the Dana 60, which was included in the A33 Track Pak and A34 Super Track Pak option groups. (Courtesy Vanguard Motor Sales)

comparison, 50–70 in fourth gear was 3.9 seconds.) We made comparison runs with and without the Air Grabber deployed and found it cut 0-30– and 0-45–mph times significantly, but we couldn't detect any difference in the quarter."

Something they could detect on the strip, and street, were higher engine speeds resulting from the 4.10:1 rear gear inside the Dana 60 rear end that was the centerpiece of the car's Code A34 Super Track Pak option group. Shuman wrote, "The car was going through the traps at the end of the quarter at close to 5,500 [rpm] in top gear, turning 99 mph. This gearing is obviously not very practical for the street, as the engine is turning more than 3,500 at 75 mph. A better choice for all-around use would be the 3.54 [rear gear] option."

Handling was what you could expect from a 3,935-pound car with a big, cast-iron V-8 mounted in front. "The Road Runner . . . tends to understeer at low speeds, but you can put it into a turn, set the attitude, and just hang in there, being quite comfortable at relatively high speeds," wrote Shuman.

He added, "The lack of power steering on our Road Runner, combined with the wide tires, made parking a chore to say the least. Power steering with any of these big-engined cars would be a good idea, as would the front-bucket-seat option. The Road Runner's bucket seats are tops, giving good lateral support, and are certainly prefera-ble to the bench seat."

The test car's lack of power steering was also noted in the *Motor Trend* feature. "The same forward weight bias that makes power steering a necessity also contributes to a tendency for the rear end to come around on hard braking, most noticeably on panic stops from 60 mph and above," Shuman noted. "All three cars exhibited this trait, but it was most pronounced in the Road Run-ner, although its stopping distances were good." Brak-ing distances were 26.1 feet from 30 mph, and 125.5 feet from 60 mph.

Shuman recorded his and other *Motor Trend* staffers' observations about this third-year Bird. "The Road Runner was the closest thing to a strictly dragstrip machine. The addition of power steering and a switch to a more realistic gear ratio would do wonders for its day-to-day drivability.

"We were a bit concerned about our particular test car's performance compared to how other simi-larly equipped Road Runners are doing, so we had the engine checked out after our bout on the dragstrip. Mopar expert Norm Thatcher diagnosed the problem as sticky valves and lifters, which he cured. He also richened the center carburetor and reset the ignition timing.

Could a hydraulic-cammed 426 Hemi run as well on the street as it did on the strip? Yes, but it took expert tuning to get the big engine to perform as intended. (Photo Courtesy David Newhardt)

"Going back to the strip, we decided to employ a few of the drag racer's tricks: We pumped up the rear tire pressure to 35 psi (Polyglas tires give better traction with higher pressure) and loosened the fan belt. The cumulative effect was evident, with the car running a best elapsed time of 14.06 [seconds] and a best speed of 101.6 [mph] in the quarter. There was a noticeable improvement in performance in the higher RPM range, thanks to Thatcher's tuning.

"All three of the vehicles tested had, to varying degrees, the performance, handling, and braking that you'd expect from a Supercar, but they were also loaded with the creature comforts you don't usually associate with the breed. Could be that we're getting into a new bag, the mature Supercar."

Mature, yes, but when loaded with options, its sticker price of

Leave it in "D" or shift the TorqueFlite automatic manually? That's a question Road Runner owners asked themselves, before figuring out their best shifting practice at their local tracks' "test-and-tune" sessions. (Photo Courtesy David Newhardt)

more than $4,000 pushed it out of the "budget muscle car" category for which it had been created.

The December 1969 issue of *Super Stock & Drag Illustrated (SSDI)* magazine hit the newsstands at around the same time. It featured a comparison dragstrip test of two new Road Runner hardtops: one powered by the 426 Hemi, the other by the 440 Six Barrel. Both cars were optioned similarly with the heavy-duty TorqueFlite automatic gearbox, the Code A32 Super Performance Axle Package with a

The Road Runner 426 Hemi delivered towering performance that put it right at the front of the muscle car pack. (Photo Courtesy Geoff Stunkard)

4.10-geared Dana 60 rear end, power steering, and power disc brakes.

SSDI staffers drove both cars from Detroit to their offices outside Washington, D.C., for a 700-mile, high-speed break-in before both cars headed to York (Pennsylvania) US-30 Dragway for on-track testing and

Through its production run, the 426 Hemi was rated at 425 hp at 5,000 rpm and 490 ft-lbs of torque at 4,000 rpm. Many dynos, however, confirmed that the figure was highly underrated, and a properly tuned Hemi could easily produce 500 hp. (Photo Courtesy David Newhardt)

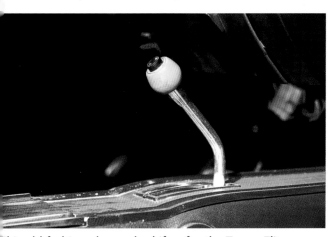

This old-fashioned console shifter for the TorqueFlite automatic transmission was in its last year of B-Body duty in 1970, to be replaced by the Slap-Stik shifter for 1971. (Photo Courtesy David Newhardt)

tuning. "As expected, there were no problems in [this] portion of the testing, except for the abominable gas mileage at cruising speeds," said author Jim McCraw. "The 4.10 gearing really made the engines churn, and mileage slipped to 10 mpg or less for the cars' first road trip. Of course, as the engines were broken in, the mileage picked up considerably."

"Considerable" is a word that also describes these test cars' weights, which SSDI gave at around 3,600 pounds for the 440 Six car and 4,000 pounds for the Hemi. Some might say that weight led to the somewhat-sluggish times on the first runs: 14.35 seconds at 101.58 mph for the 440 Six Barrel and 14.31 seconds at 104.65 mph for the Hemi.

As with the Motor Trend test, SSDI performed some trackside between-run tweaks to both cars, aided by Bill Stiles, a York, Pennsylvania Plymouth drag racer and speed-shop owner. For the 440 Six Barrel Bird, he reset the ignition timing from 38 to 33 degrees, which improved the ET and speed to 13.76 seconds at 102.85 mph. He also flushed out and refilled the radiator, sprayed the front of the radiator with water, and removed the air-filter element. In addition, he opened the Air Grabber manually so that it was wide open during the run-up in speed but with a slightly slower ET, at 13.81 seconds at 102.85 mph. Shifting the Torque-Flite at 5,000 rpm instead of 5,500 rpm gave the quickest ET with the 440 Six at 13.65 seconds, but the trap speed was almost unchanged at 102.62 mph.

Stiles lowered the Hemi to 14.18 seconds at 104.65 mph on its second warm-up run with no modifications, and then set to work. A change in driving technique, where he smoothed it off the starting line the first 25 to 40 feet before stomping on the throttle and opening all eight of the Hemi's carburetor barrels, resulted in a quickest run of 13.58 seconds at 104.89 mph.

A fresh watering of the Hemi only picked up .03 second. Stiles then boosted the tire pressures to 32 psi, replaced the spark plugs with an identical set of Champion N-10-Y plugs, removed the air-filter element,

If ever there was a race-ready shifter on a Chrysler manual transmission, it had to be the Hurst Pistol Grip that debuted for 1970. The long shifter handle was used by the factory on 1970 B-Body Dodges and Plymouths only, owing to the shifter location relative to the driver's seat. (Photo Courtesy David Newhardt)

flushed and refilled the radiator, and shifted at 6,500 rpm instead of 5,500 rpm. That brought the ET down to 13.48 seconds and the speed up to 107.27 mph. Two more runs with no further modifications to the Hemi car led to a best ET and speed of 13.37 seconds at 107.52 mph.

Author McCraw noted, "Even with a hydraulic cam, the Hemi is a superior engine that responds to even the smallest tune job. Whether the Hemi is worth the extra money and extra weight over the 440 Six Barrel for four-tenths and 3½ mph remains a question answerable only by buyers of 1970 Road Runners."

However, the two Birds weren't without their problems. "The finish on both cars was not up to snuff," said McCraw. "Maybe because they were rather hurriedly built as road-test cars, maybe because the people who built them were not feeling well, but whatever the reason, the cars weren't built right. Both leaked water terribly during automatic car wash visits.

"The seatback latch escutcheons were loose on all four buckets and caused a lot of smashed hands before the backs would release. The disc brakes on the [440 Six] wedge car squealed and moaned because the disc run-out was excessive. And the Dust Swirl side trim on both cars was out of alignment by as much as a quarter inch at the door/body junctions."

Nevertheless, the heavy-duty powertrains in both cars received praise. "The engine and drivetrain components on our twin Birds cannot be faulted," said McCraw. "They ran hot, straight, and normal the whole time (and by normal, I mean normal for what they were. Both were temperamental cold starters because of multiple carburetor setups and smog settings, but once fired, no overheating or balkiness was noted). The TorqueFlite transmissions were so solid and quick shifting that one of our testers received a citation for squealing the tires when in fact the transmission had done it automatically on a half-throttle 1-2 shift."

The *SSDI* double-drag-test feature concluded, "These cars are respectable, if not outstanding, performers right off the showroom floor. They are to be considered decent handlers despite their weights (3,600 to 4,000 pounds, depending on scales, load, and accessories). They sell like gangbusters, but this year we think the stylists have gone off the deep end with the dust-swirl business and the air-inlet door. (Thank goodness they're not standard.) Time could have been well spent on designing leak-proof doors, windows, and trunks, which these cars have needed since their introduction, not to mention a little more classy interior finish (plastic panels and Philips-head screws, like brown shoes with a black suit, just don't make it).

"As for the Road Runner's performance capabilities within the realm of Pure Stock [class drag racing], a future issue will carry a similar side-by-side comparison on these cars with allowable mods, and possibly still another with some more expensive work in them. Then we'll see just how rapid the Rapid Transit System really is."

Unfortunately, that second side-by-side feature never appeared in *SSDI* during the 1970 model year.

CHAPTER 6

PROMOTION, MARKETING AND SALES

Chrysler built just 827 droptop Road Runners for 1970. This is one of just 34 equipped with the 440 Six Barrel engine option. Special parts for the 440 included large-port cylinder heads, which were shared with the Road Runner's standard 383, as well as high-performance cast-iron exhaust manifolds on each side, which went up and over the exhaust ports. (Photo Courtesy David Newhardt)

It's easy to say that Plymouth's Rapid Transit System for 1970 was a copy of Dodge's performance marketing efforts with the Scat Pack, which arrived on the scene two years earlier, for 1968. But Dodge's "bumblebee-striped" cars were built at first on the mid-size B-Body and compact A-Body platforms, with the new E-Body Challenger R/T and Challenger T/A joining the Pack for 1970. (Plymouth, by contrast, included its full-size Sport Fury GT in the Rapid Transit System.) By then, Dodge wasn't actively promoting the big Polara and Monaco models' performance; the only one that could hold a candle to the performance Challengers, Super Bee, Charger R/T, and Coronet R/T was the police-package Polara sedan. Its 140-mph top speed

and reputation for ruggedness helped give it the name "The Corvette Killer," for the way it survived high-speed pursuits (especially in California) while the Corvettes, Porsches, Ferraris, and other fast cars that dared challenge it blew up while running at more than 100 mph for mile after mile.

There were some interesting similarities, however, aimed directly at the age 18 to 25 segment of the new-car market. Like Dodge, Plymouth sponsored Performance Clinics in conjunction with the personal appearances of one of the top drag racing teams, Sox & Martin. Since 1964, Buddy Martin's mechanical skill and Ronnie Sox' quick reflexes behind the wheel (plus his legendary ability to shift the A-833 4-speed transmission

The Rapid Transit System, explained by Plymouth. Note the "big names," including Buddy Martin and Ronnie Sox (wearing Plymouth Racing Team jackets) and their Super Stock 1969 Plymouth Road Runner; Don "The Snake" Prudhomme and Tom "Mongoose" McEwen; plus Super Stock drag racer Don Grotheer and USAC stock car ace Norm Nelson, the latter two shown at speed. Guess who's missing? Richard Petty. He announced his return to Plymouth after this brochure was published. (Courtesy Fiat Chrysler Automobiles)

quickly under full acceleration) made them regular winners in class racing. Race fans packed the grandstands when Sox & Martin matched raced other A/Factory Experimental or early Funny Cars. In many cases, they match raced Dodge's "Dandy" Dick Landy and Mopar enthusiasts had the chance to attend either brand's local Performance Clinic, or both. (Also appearing at Plymouth's "Supercar Clinics" was Plymouth Pro Stock/Super Stock racer Don Grotheer, whose participation enabled Plymouth to hold two clinics on the same weekend, near where both teams competed.)

Sox & Martin, like Landy, switched to production-based Stock and Super Stock racing in 1967, and were among the pioneers who raced in NHRA's new Pro Stock class when it began at the season-opening Winternationals at Pomona, California, in February 1970.

By then, word of the Rapid Transit System had reached all corners of the country and it helped drive

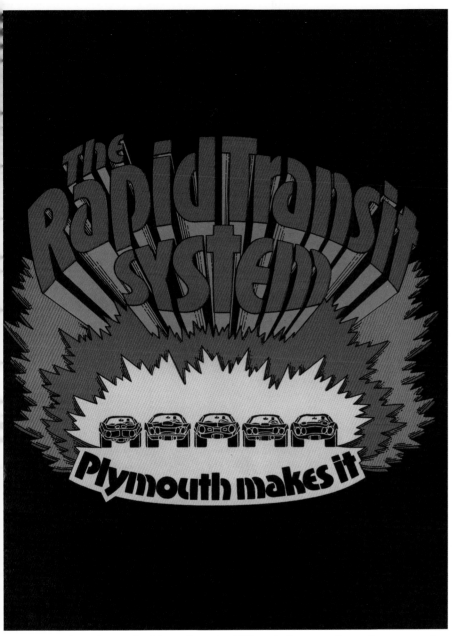

In the year that Plymouth debuted its Rapid Transit System of muscle cars small and large, more intra-Plymouth competition for the Road Runner than the GTX appeared. This is a 1970 'Cuda, a Mustang-fighter built on a shortened version of the 1971 B-Body platform, and which could have siphoned some sales from Road Runner. (Courtesy Fiat Chrysler Automobiles)

traffic to Chrysler-Plymouth showrooms. There, prospective buyers found a dedicated Rapid Transit System brochure, whose text began: "Those of us at Plymouth who design and build high-performance cars have been inspired to go beyond just offering cars with big engines, good suspensions, great brakes, and fat tires.

"We now have a system. An integrated program. It's mathematics rather than numbers. Oceanography rather than salt water. It's a total concept in high-performance transportation that combines the lessons learned in competition, an information network, people who understand high performance, trick parts, and great products."

Front and center among those great products was the Road Runner. You couldn't miss its appearance in the Rapid Transit System brochure: a Banana Yellow coupe wearing the new-for-1970 "dust trail" stripes and Air Grabber hood scoop (open in the brochure's two-page photo.) "Thanks to the System, America's favorite Bird is more than a put-on," read the headline. "The Ultimate put-on.

"That was the way they described Road Runner when it was first introduced in September 1967.

"What? A car with a horn that goes 'Beep-Beep' instead of 'honk-honk' and uses gawky little cartoon birds for insignia. The very idea.

Road Runner Coupe

Road Runner. Thanks to the System, America's favorite bird is more than a put-on.

The ultimate put-on.

That was the way they described Road Runner when it was first introduced in September of 1967.

What? A car with a horn that goes "Beep-Beep" instead of Honk-Honk and uses gawky little cartoon birds for insignia. The very idea.

Where were the usual symbols of Supercar virility? Like maybe ermine carpeting or lightning bolts flashing from your hood-mounted gas gauge? Road Runner? You're kidding. Haw-Haw!

But it was no put-on. Road Runner was the country's first no-nonsense high-performance car. Its theme was race-car simple: a rugged two-door coupe, deliberately devoid of interior and exterior frills, with maximum attention on engine, driveline, suspension and brakes. In turn, that meant the price could be held to a minimum, and for the first time, the young people of this country could afford the kind of car they wanted—brand new.

Haw-Haw. In its first two years, Road Runner sold well over 100,000 units. Last year it was named Car of the Year by Motor Trend.

The 1970 version reflects both its original product philosophy and its own incredible popularity.

The 383 cubic inch engine with its 440 cubic inch heads, cam and carburetion is still standard equipment. The same goes for the heavy-duty suspension, special 11" heavy-duty brakes and heavy-duty rear axle. The only change is that we've substituted a floor-mounted 3-speed in place of the usual 4-speed, which is now available as an option.

So much for tradition. Over the years, we've expanded Road Runner's model lineup to include a hardtop and a convertible as well as offering options such as fancy interiors, consoles and the like. To give it what our research people call "broadened market appeal." The 1970 Road Runner offers the biggest list of add-on goodies ever.

Of these, perhaps the most newsworthy is a 440 cu. in. V-8 fed by three Holley 2-barrel carbs. Performance, as you might expect, is positively mind-expanding and nearly equals the Street Hemi, even though the "6-bbl." is priced many skins less. And speaking of the Hemi, you can throw away your feeler gauges—hydraulic lifters are now standard.

In addition, there's a new Air Grabber induction system available. Touch a switch on the dash and—Zap!—the scoop raises up out of the hood like a NIKE launcher.

Beyond that, there are trick options like dust trails that span the length of the body, new flat-black hood striping, a set of low-cost road wheels and extra-wide F-60 rubber.

Funny about those guys who laughed at the first Road Runner. They're so silent lately. Haw-Haw.

6   7

What better way to show off a Road Runner in the Rapid Transit System brochure than with a 440 Six Barrel coupe finished in one of the new High Impact colors (Lemon Twist), with the new Air Grabber cold-air intake and Dust Trail: side stripes! (Courtesy Fiat Chrysler Automobiles)

"Where were the usual symbols of Supercar virility? Like maybe ermine carpeting or lightning bolts flashing from your hood-mounted gas gauge? Road Runner? You're kidding. Haw-Haw."

(Did you notice the not-so subtle jab at Pontiac's GTO there, referring to its long option list, which drove its sticker price to well over $4,000, and its available hood-mounted tachometer?)

The brochure continued, "But it was no put-on. Road Runner was the country's first no-nonsense high-performance car. Its theme was race-car simple: A rugged two-door coupe, deliberately devoid of interior and exterior frills, with maximum attention on engine, driveline, suspension, and brakes. In turn, that meant the price could be held to a minimum, and for the first time, the young people of this country could afford the kind of car they wanted, brand new.

"Haw-Haw. In its first two years, the Road Runner sold well over 100,000 units, Last year, it was named Car of the Year by Motor Trend."

The rest of the text describes the 1970 Bird, its standard and available features: "The 1970 Road Runner

Chrysler-Plymouth dealers hoped to improve on the Road Runner's 1969 sales figures (including 2,123 convertibles), but a saturated market and rising insurance costs were two factors that held the final tally of the droptop for 1970 to only 824. This example owned by Henry Liebman is one of 429 383 TorqueFlite-equipped 1970 Road Runner convertibles, the most popular of its available powertrain choices. (Least popular? The 426 Hemi 4-speed, as only one was built.)

offers the biggest list of add-on goodies ever," read the body copy and concluded, "Funny about those guys who laughed at the first Road Runner.

"They're so silent lately.

"Haw-Haw."

However, one name, one familiar number, and one color scheme were missing from the Rapid Transit System's brochures, print ads, and showroom displays at the start of the 1970 model year. They were Petty, 43, and Petty Blue.

Why?

During the later stages of the 1968 NASCAR Grand National Championship season, Richard Petty (a two-time series champ who'd dominated it in 1967) was frustrated with his #43's performance at Daytona and NASCAR's other high-speed ovals, despite the 1968 Road Runner being one of the most "tricked out" cars he had ever raced. So, when word of the

aerodynamically-superior 1969 Dodge Charger 500 came out of Highland Park that June, he and his father, Lee Petty (a past Grand National champ who'd run the family race operation as a business long before the end of his driving career), made it known to Chrysler's racing operations that they wanted to run a Charger 500 for 1969. According to allpar.com, they asked Chrysler twice and were turned down twice. They were told that, as a Plymouth driver, it would not be possible.

In response, they said, "We're driving Fords for 1969," and made a one-year deal with Ford to run a Petty Blue #43 Torino Talladega on the high-speed tracks and a regular-production-based Torino Cobra fastback on the short ovals and dirt tracks. They even won their first race for Ford, at Riverside, California.

This did not go down well in Highland Park. According to allpar.com, "Chrysler President Lynn Townsend took the announcement in rare form by reverting to his un-corporate self, which had earned him the nickname "Flamethrower." He was spitting bolts between sheets of hot flaming invectives. He wanted Petty back in a Chrysler product, and said, "By damn; somebody down there in engineering and racing better see to it right now!"

By June 1969 (around the time that Plymouth's Rapid Transit System brochures were headed to the printer), Richard Petty agreed to drive Plymouth's counterpart to the ultra-aerodynamic Dodge Charger Daytona for 1970, the Road Runner Superbird.

Within days of unveiling the 1970 Plymouth lineup, Rapid Transit System ads appeared, showing Richard Petty and the entire Petty Enterprises crew around their newly-completed #43 Superbird. Above the headline, it read, "The obvious reason why Richard Petty came back."

The 1970 Plymouth Rapid Transit System brochure's introductory text concluded, "Finally the Rapid Transit System is common sense on your part. You know, when you want to really turn it on, turn it on at a sanctioned strip.

"This year, give the Rapid Transit System careful consideration."

IN SCALE: ROAD RUNNERS FOR THE YOUNG

Away from the track, those not yet of driving age were among those targeted by the Rapid Transit System. The 1970 RTS brochure had this to say about those Plymouth devotees who were months or years away from their drivers' licenses: "The System even has a piece of the action for beginners. Let's say you're still a few years away from a driver's license, but that hasn't dampened your enthusiasm for cars. Your favorite cartoon is Road Runner, your favorite car is Road Runner, and you only wish your driveway was a couple of miles long. Well, maybe you're not old enough to drive, but you sure can wear a Plymouth racing jacket [like the ones Ronnie Sox and Buddy Martin are pictured wearing]. And you can also pick or send for a handful of our

decals, stickers, catalogs and brochures. And go to free Sox & Martin and Don Grotheer Supercar Clinics."

Those Plymouth racing jackets also served another purpose for the not-yet-driving set, of which I was a proud member in the fall of 1969. Those who had them wore them when they made their annual brochure-collecting run to their home town's Dealership Row, and served to annoy the Ford and Chevrolet

Jo-Han Models' 1/25-scale of the 1970 Plymouth Road Runner dazzled kit buyers in late 1969 and early 1970, thanks to its vivid box art and detailed (for the time) contents. (Photo Courtesy Ken Schmidt)

Just as in 1969, Jo-Han used a vivid, "pop-art" illustration atop its Road Runner kit box. (Photo by Claes Ericsson)

dealers once their presence was detected on their lots. Those kids then took off running not unlike the cartoon bird, yelling "BEEP BEEP!" but (unfortunately) not causing the sidewalk or road under their feet to "ribbon" like the bird did on the two-lane roads of Chuck Jones' stylized American Southwest.

The start of the new model year was also the time that the makers of 1/25-scale replicas of the new cars hit the hobby shops, toy stores, department stores, and five-and-dimes across the land. To them, one of the makers of the kits (and assembled "promo" scale models in factory colors) had a name as familiar as Plymouth and Chrysler itself: Jo-Han Models.

John Haenle made the first 1/25-scale Chrysler-product replica in 1955 at his Jo-Han Models plant on Detroit's near east side. The miniature was a detailed, factory-colors model of the De Soto Firedome sedan that became a sensation in the toy and hobby world with its bright two-tone factory colors; sparkling "chrome" bumpers, grille, and wheel covers (actually, vacuum-metallized plastic using powdered aluminum); and proportions and accurate engraving of the "Firedome" and "De Soto" scripts on the body that could only come by Jo-Han's tool and die makers using Chrysler's official factory blueprints to guide them.

These were produced under arrangement with Chrysler, who bought a quantity of the models for dealer giveaways as a part of their licensing deal to use the blueprints, which also included funds for Jo-Han to make the molds ("tools").

For 1956, Jo-Han's model-car lineup expanded to include Plymouth and Dodge, and for 1957, it also included Chrysler. (Imperial, and later Valiant, were licensed to one of Jo-Han's competitors, Scale Model Products, SMP, which entered into a joint venture with the company that pioneered injection-molded plastic annual scale car models, AMT Corporation, in the late 1950s. Originally called Aluminum Model Toys, AMT and SMP eventually merged in 1961.)

The year 1958 saw AMT and SMP offer unassembled versions of their annual models, with a "tree" of customizing and racing parts. Young builders could assemble it as a factory-stock replica, a show-stopping custom, or a competition car. (Many times, they used all of the parts in the box!)

Jo-Han joined the annual "3-in-1" kit market for 1959, and like the merged AMT, eventually began offering them with opening hoods and detailed engines. For 1964, details in the Plymouth kits also included a full NASCAR-style roll cage, Race Hemi engine, racing wheels/tires and other parts, and a set of #43 decals to make a replica of the car in which Richard Petty won his first Daytona 500 in 1964. (This kit proved to be so popular that it was re-issued the next year with Petty box art, during Chrysler's NASCAR boycott of 1965, and was reissued several more times beginning in 1968.)

That was the last B-Body Plymouth by Jo-Han until 1969, when the company tooled up to produce the Road Runner, which could be built as a coupe or hardtop, as well as the GTX hardtop. (A GTX convertible was planned for a spring 1969 release by Jo-Han, but it was canceled before it entered production.)

Both the Road Runner and GTX kits contained vivid box artwork, borrowing from Plymouth's print ads of the time.

For 1970, Road Runner and GTX kits returned from Jo-Han, updated with the new 1970 styling, as well as new features, including the Pistol Grip shifter, Rallye dash cluster, and high-back front bucket seats. However, due to Richard Petty's departure for Ford, there were no #43 Petty markings on the enclosed decal sheet, just a generic #25. (That year's Ford Torino GT fastback kit from AMT, which also boasted a NASCAR stock car version, didn't have any Petty numbers or markings either.)

Once again, the building choices were factory stock with a 426 Hemi topped by a functional Air Grabber scoop, a 4-speed, bucket seats, and five-spoke wheels; a custom with stylized front and rear parts that fit in place of the stock bumpers, grille, and taillights; and the above-mentioned stock car racing version.

A hallmark of Jo-Han's models was the exacting detail on nameplates and trim items such as the bird itself (a very detailed running bird was molded in, in the exact same spots you found it on the actual car), plus you could see all the markings on the dashboard gauges and the dial on the in-dash scale AM radio. You could tell what radio station the tool and die maker liked to listen to, by where the tuner on the kit dashboard's radio dial was located!

Unfortunately, the Road Runner was not offered in fully-assembled promo form for dealer giveaways in 1970, or available to the toy and hobby market. The GTX was the only B-Body Plymouth offered in factory-built form, as it had been for 1969.

The last year for Jo-Han to make the midsize Plymouths was 1970. For 1971, Plymouth moved all its promo and kit business to another competitor, Model Products Corporation (MPC) in Mount Clemens, Michigan. Started in 1964 by AMT founder George Toteff (who'd left AMT to start this company), the company had been making Dodge's kits and promos since 1965.

As the 1970s progressed, the pool of available kit builders diminished, as those who had been modelers grew to drivers' license age and turned to full-size cars. Also, the pool of potential new builders was shrinking, with the decline in the U.S. birth rate after 1964. As a result, the kit-makers fortunes suffered; none more than Jo-Han, whose line of annuals shrank every year until it made its last new annual tool for 1977 (the Cadillac Coupe deVille). Jo-Han reissued some of its earlier kits under the "USA Oldies" banner in the mid-1970s, but the 1970 Road Runner was not among them; the tool was converted back to a 1969 body, but the incorrect 1970 seats and dash remained.

In later years, when Jo-Han's Detroit plant was ravaged by thieves who stole expensive and difficult-to-reproduce metal parts from the stock of tools, those affected kits could no longer be issued without expensive restoration work, which Jo-Han could no longer afford, especially as it went through ownership changes in the 1980s and 1990s. Chrysler likely didn't have any funds for that purpose either, especially after its 1980 federally-assisted "bailout."

It is feared that the Jo-Han 1969–1970 Plymouth Road Runner tool is now either lost or not enough of it remains for the current ownership of Jo-Han Models to reissue it without a very expensive restoration. That's because the tools for model kits cost from $50,000 to $100,000 in the early 1970s to produce and cost much more than that in later years.

That makes the surviving Jo-Han kits, either in built-up or in (rare) unbuilt form, command premium prices from online vendors such as SpotlightHobbies.com (as well as eBay) and at model car shows where vendors sell their stocks of unbuilt kits, as well as promos, in either new-in-original-box condition or "used."

In recent years, Revell/Monogram has produced a new-tool 1970 Road Runner kit, with a more-detailed chassis that includes separate suspension and exhaust components, plus a much higher parts count than in the Jo-Han kits. They're intended for many of those original builders, who are now much older, with better model-building skills, yet still have the desire to build the car of their dreams in scale, even if the radio dial in the dashboard in them no longer shows Detroit rock-and-roll radio stations such as Detroit's "Keener 13."

ROAD RUNNER RTS CARAVAN

The Road Runner RTS Caravan concept was an audacious evolution of the production Road Runner, built for display at new-car shows from coast to coast as an attention-getter for the 1970 Road Runner (and the entire Plymouth lineup).

The attention-grabbing show car featured a bold and unique styling package with a distinctive tri-color custom paint job. Although it was a daring step in a different direction, it also shared many styling cues from the production model, such as the Air Grabber hood scoop, hood pins, and a similar-looking grille but with square headlights.

In back, the rear-quarter panels were flared outward 4 inches over the rear wheels to accommodate the massive wheel/tire combination that went inside. (The technique of "tubbing" a car for increased tire clearance by replacing the stock rear fender wells with larger "tubs" had not yet begun.) Those quarters also saw their simulated side scoops sculpted into functional scoops, with a longer and thinner inlet than seen on the stock quarters. The rear spoiler is instantly recognizable, but the specialized design was molded into the top of the quarter panels, two support pillars suspend the middle element, and the trunk opens conventionally.

From the first look, it becomes apparent that this concept car was also a radical departure from the production model. The Chrysler 300 side-marker lights replaced the standard Road Runner markers. Electric solenoid door openers were installed, which in turn led to the "shaving" of the stock door handles and the door and trunk lock cylinders for a smoother overall look.

At this Bird's tail end, stylists created an eye-catching package with the taillights flowing gracefully across the entire rear panel. The trunk provided a backlight for the taillights, which are adorned with Road Runner graphics.

On the sides, the large Road Runner graphic and "dust trail" that extends to the rear-quarter panel is painted on each door. But changes were not relegated to just the exterior; this show car was as much of an eye-grabber inside as it was on the outside.

Thus, the RTS Caravan received the luxury-appointed GTX interior, and that included a six-way adjustable driver's seat, woodgrain trim, and power windows. With styling this impressive, it deserved a powerful engine to match the radical exterior. That meant the new-for-1970 440 Six Barrel, backed by a 4-speed with a 3.54-geared Dana 60 rear end.

SALES DROP: DON'T BLAME WILE E. COYOTE

Despite all that the third-year Road Runner had going for it in the way of available body styles and options, 1970 sales were a major disappointment. One year after 88,415 Birds rolled out of the nation's

The upscale and luxurious interior features high-back bucket seats with a manual six-way adjustment for the driver's side, woodgrain trim, power windows, and custom carpeting. (Photo Courtesy David Newhardt)

The Air Grabber hood scoop was fitted to potent engines and a 440 with a 4-speed A-833 powered the Road Runner RTS. A Dana 3.54 rear end transmitted power to rear tires. (Photo Courtesy David Newhardt)

The Road Runner RTS featured audacious yet attractive styling that was a bold departure from the production car. But of course, concept and show cars are meant to generate excitement and tease the imagination. The bold tri-color paint job, graphics and styling were certainly unique. (Photo Courtesy David Newhardt)

Chrysler-Plymouth dealers, the sales tally dropped 51 percent to only 41,484 for 1970. That included 15,716 coupes (down from 33,743 in 1969), 24,944 hardtops (compared with 1969's 48,549), and just 824 convertibles (in contrast to 2,123 the year before).

More than a few reasons explained the sales drop, including the maturing of those young new-car buyers who'd bought Road Runners and other muscle cars over the previous several years, but who now needed something more practical for daily use, something with room for a growing family. They were more likely to look for a sedan, station wagon, or window van rather than a muscle car, with their existing tire-fryer giving way to a regular-gas grocery-getter instead of a mature muscle car

The Road Runner RTS featured square headlights, rather than the round headlights found in the 1970 grille. Locking hood pins among other equipment signaled to everyone that it was ready for high-performance service. (Photo Courtesy David Newhardt)

The Road Runner graphic was not a subtle styling cue on RTS Road Runners. As you can see, the Road Runner and dust tail graphic adorns the doors and rear quarter panels. (Photo Courtesy David Newhardt)

The 1970 model year also marked a point of saturation in the muscle car segment of the new-car market. That year, every U.S. automobile brand except Cadillac, Lincoln, Chrysler, and Imperial had at least one midsize 300+hp muscle car in its lineup. Even American Motors, which had long eschewed quick-and-fast cars in favor of those whose performance was measured in miles per dollar instead of miles per hour, now had a boldly trimmed AMC Rebel Machine available in its midsize Rebel lineup. It was powered by a 390-ci version of AMC's potent small-block V-8 and had a heavy-duty suspension system front and rear that was the basis for the chassis that AMC later used under police-package Matador sedans from 1972 to 1974. Initial Rebel Machines were painted white with red and blue trim, much as the 1969 Hurst SC/Rambler hardtops were, but AMC offered the Rebel Machine in regular-production colors as the year went on.

Not only was there competition from AMC, Chevrolet, and Ford, but also from Pontiac, whose GTO had defined the midsize muscle car upon its 1964 introduction. In 1969, the Pontiac lineup had expanded to include The Judge hardtop and convertible models. Oldsmobile's muscle cars were the 4-4-2, Rallye 350, and Hurst-upgraded Hurst/Olds; Buick had its Skylark GS 400 and GSX; Mercury's long-nosed Cyclone and Cyclone Spoiler were counterparts to Ford's Torino GT and Torino Cobra models; and Dodge's Scat Pack lineup for 1970 included the Coronet R/T, Coronet Super Bee, and Charger R/T.

Three new Plymouths (Duster 340, 'Cuda, and the mid-year AAR 'Cuda) were available in high-output form and also competed with the Road Runner for buyers' attention. The 426 Hemi was installed in the E-Body 'Cuda, and the E-Body shared its A-pillars, windshield, substructure and cowl/firewall with the Road Runner and all other B-Body cars from 1971 onward, and thus it had increased appeal to performance buyers. In its first year as a separate Barracuda series instead of as an option group, the 'Cuda drew 18,880 buyers for the hardtop and 635 for the convertible. Power was pulled from Chrysler's range of high-output engines: from the 340 small-block to the 383- and 440-inch B/RB big-blocks to the 426 Hemi.

New styling, at least from the cowl rearward, was also the A-Body Duster two-door's hallmark. When it was combined with the high-revving 340 and either the A-833 4-speed or 727 TorqueFlite automatic transmission, the resulting Duster 340 was a giant killer on the street and on the track. It drew 24,817 buyers in its first year.

The Road Runner's flowing rear deck, roof, and hood line come into view. The exquisitely styled rear taillight panel features the Road Runner icon, and the rear wing uprights have been integrated into the rear quarter panels. (Photo Courtesy David Newhardt)

The Road Runner's hardtop model was a midyear addition in 1968, and was the line's biggest seller in 1969 and 1970. From its High Impact paint color and Dust Trail stripes (and the Air Grabber hood scoop), this is what Mopar performance enthusiasts think of when the 1970 Bird comes to mind. (Photo Courtesy David Newhardt)

Combine the 1970 Duster 340s and 'Cudas and they add up to 44,332 high-performance A-Body and E-Body Plymouths. However, that is less than the nearly 47,000-car drop in Road Runner sales compared to 1969's final tally. That leads to the biggest factor affecting not only Road Runner sales, but sales of every American-built high-performance car in 1970: insurance.

The companies that wrote and sold collision and liability insurance for passenger cars were alarmed by the amount of money they were paying in claims relating to crashes involving muscle cars. They raised rates for high-performance cars, especially those owned by drivers under age 25 with a history of speeding tickets and other moving violations. They also added surcharges for items such as floor-mounted shifters, tachometers, bucket seats, raised-white-letter tires, and factory wheel treatments that weren't a steel full-wheel cover or hubcap on a steel rim. Full-wheel covers were also a headache for insurers due to their loss by theft or from a wheel flexing under hard cornering so much that its cover dismounted and rolled away.

The result was monthly insurance premiums for cars such as the Road Runner that were as much as or more than the car's monthly payment if insurance was available at all. When the premiums were combined with the not-exactly-high incomes of the prospective buyers in the targeted market (namely, men ages 18 to 25 years), many buyers decided that they simply couldn't afford to insure one.

Add in a recession that the American economy experienced for much of 1970, and you can see why Road Runner sales dropped significantly from 1969 to 1970.

oes the thought of a third-year Bird roosting in your garage interest you? As with any used car, it pays to look around. In the case of a specific car with collector appeal such as the 1970 Plymouth Road Runner, it starts with finding one that is indeed a Road Runner and not a Belvedere or Satellite that's been transformed into one.

Decoding its vehicle identification number (VIN) is the first step in establishing a car's identity.

During the 1970 model year, Chrysler Corporation passenger cars used a 13-character VIN. It denoted the

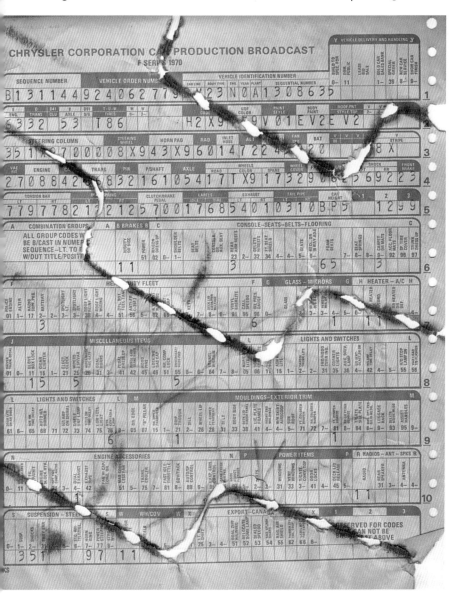

Along with the fender tag and VIN tag, Broadcast Sheets provided another way to identify the factory-installed equipment on a 1970 Road Runner. Chrysler's assembly plants used these sheets to tell the line workers what components should go on a given car as it passed their workstations. The impression of the seat springs shows that this one was tucked under the passenger-side front seat. These sheets may also be located under the rear seat or in the trunk. (Photo Courtesy Vanguard Motor Sales)

75

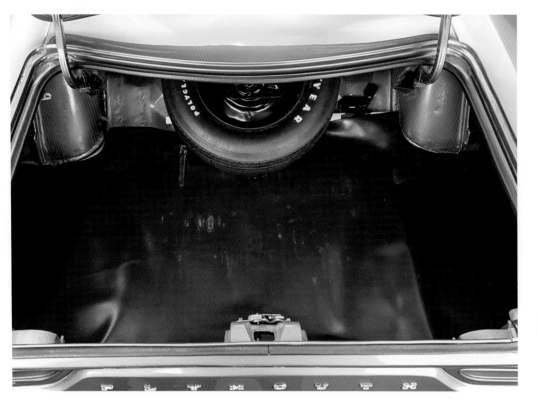

When inspecting a potential purchase, the trunk deserves more than just a cursory look. Water leaking from the Dutchman panel aft of the rear window can lead to corrosion of that panel and to the trunk floor beneath it. Pull back any trunk mats to ensure that the floor underneath it is still intact. (Photo Courtesy Vanguard Motor Sales)

car line, price class, body style, engine, assembly plant, and build-sequence number (serial number) on a metal tag affixed to the dashboard's lower driver-side corner (visible through the windshield). The door tag in the driver-side door opening stated the car's compliance with applicable federal safety and emissions-control standards as of the date that the car was built. The stamped-metal fender tag affixed to the driver-side front fenderwell under the hood listed the engine, transmission, color, trim, and option codes for that car, as well as its date of final assembly.

That year, Chrysler also stamped a car's partial VIN or sequence order (SO) number in two locations, the radiator upper-core support bar under the hood and the driver's side of the deck-lid seal lip, where eight characters from the car's VIN appeared.

The SO number also appeared on the fender tag, next to the code for the car's final assembly date.

INSPECTING A ROAD RUNNER

Before buying any car that's nearly 50 years old, a detailed inspection is in order to see how well it's stood up after years of rain, snow, road salt, sunlight, barn storage, or any factor that might affect its condition.

Even though Chrysler used a thorough, seven-step anti-corrosion process before painting, rust is a big problem on 1970-vintage Plymouths, especially those driven regularly in places where the roads were salted to de-ice them every winter. Trouble-prone areas include the trailing edges of the front and rear wheel openings, rocker panels, front and rear floorpans, trunk floor, and the "Dutchman" panel between the rear window and trunk lid on coupes and hardtops.

Improperly installed weatherstripping, or weatherstripping not installed at all (as in the case of the

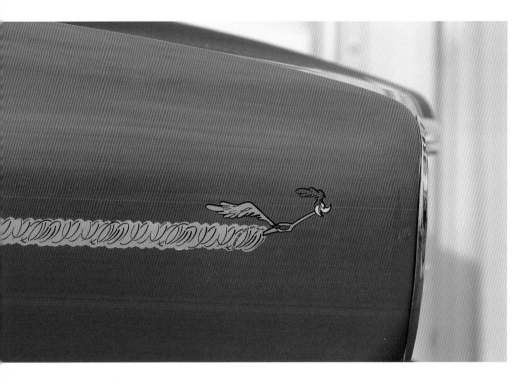

The iconic and instantly recognizable Road Runner graphic adorned one of Plymouth's most remarkable muscle cars of the era.

SSDI test cars mentioned previously) led to inadequate sealing against rain and snow that caused floorpan and trunk-floor rust. Even though a car may not have visible rust, it may have rust hidden under the trunk mat and carpets because of those floor material absorbing leaking water and soaking through to the bare metal.

If the car has been restored or had major metal repairs, the quality of the work also deserves scrutiny. Here are some questions you need to answer. Are all the body panels aligned evenly, with even gaps? Do the doors and windows open and close without binding? Were the body repairs performed using steel (original or reproduction Unibody parts such as quarter panels, rocker panels, and trunk floors, as well as smaller patch panels) or filler pastes such as Bondo-brand plastic filler?

Other areas of scrutiny include the engine and powertrain, electrical system, interior and exterior trim and paint, heater/defroster, and air conditioning (if the car was so equipped).

If you're going to invest the money that a good-condition or better 1970 Road Runner brings on the collector-car market, my advice is to buy the best car you can afford. Just as you would with a potential daily driver, make sure that it's in top condition and that its combination of features, colors, and price are what you are looking for and can afford.

If, instead, you want to turn a plain 1970 Belvedere, Satellite, or Sport Satellite into the Road Runner you always wanted (or if you want to turn a 383-powered Road Runner into the 426 Hemi–powered Bird of your dreams), make sure that you have the funds and the time to invest to get the job(s) done correctly and done correctly the first time.

Either way, as soon as that Bird is yours, you'll be like Chuck Jones' cartoon creation, for whom just running down the road is his idea of having fun. Especially after you hear another bird sound, that high-pitched song of the Chrysler gear-reduction starter motor, dubbed the Highland Park Hummingbird by Mopar lovers, and that big-power engine under the hood firing up!

77

SPECIFICATIONS

The following specifications appeared in *AMA Specifications—Passenger Car* (issued July 1, 1969; revised March 5, 1970).

Body	
RM21	Coupe
RM23	Hardtop
RM27	Convertible
Dimensions	**Inches**
Overall length	204.1
Wheelbase	116
Front track	59.7
Rear track	59.2
Maximum width	76.4
Overall height	53.0 (coupe and hardtop), 54.1 (convertible)
Front headroom	37.3 (coupe and hardtop), 39.3* (convertible)
Front legroom	41.8
Front shoulder room	58.0
Front hip room	60.6
Rear headroom	36.7 (coupe and hardtop), 37.2* (convertible)
Rear legroom	33.4 (coupe and hardtop), 34.0 (convertible)
Rear shoulder room	57.3 (coupe and hardtop), 50.4** (convertible)
Rear hip room	60.0 (coupe and hardtop), 48.6 (convertible)
Trunk, usable luggage capacity	15.9 cubic feet
Fuel-tank capacity	19 gallons

* Measured with the top up. With the top down, headroom is virtually unlimited.

** The convertible top's hydraulic cylinders intrude upon rear seat space, leading to reduced dimensions here.

Curb Weight (pounds)	
Body Type (These figures are with 383 and TorqueFlite automatic transmission.)	
Coupe	3,610
Hardtop	3,640
Convertible	3,780
Component (For each of these accessories add this number of pounds.)	
4-speed transmission	37
Airtemp air conditioning	115
Power steering	39
Power brakes	9
Radio	7

Curb Weight (pounds)

Console	22
Undercoating	35

Engines

Standard Road Runner 383

Displacement	383 ci
Bore x stroke	4.25 x 3.38 inches
Cylinder block/cylinder head material	Cast iron
Carburetion, 1x4-barrel	With manual transmission: Holley R-4367A (49-state), Holley R-4217A (California only) With TorqueFlite automatic and A/C: Holley R-4368A (49-state), Holley R-4218A (California only) With TorqueFlite, but without A/C: Holley R-4369A (50-state)
Pistons	Cast-aluminum alloy
Compression ratio	9.5:1
Crankshaft	Drop-forged steel
Valves	2.08 inches (intake) 1.74 inches (exhaust)
Valve lifters	Hydraulic
Exhaust system	Dual
Horsepower (factory advertised)	335 at 5,200 rpm
Torque (factory advertised)	425 ft-lbs at 3,400 rpm
Fuel required	Premium

Optional 440 Six Barrel

Displacement	440 ci
Bore and stroke	4.32 x 3.75 inches
Cylinder block/cylinder head material	Cast iron
Carburetion, 3x2-barrel	Front: Holley R-4382A (49-state), Holley R-4175A (California only) Center (manual transmission): Holley R-4375A (49-state), Holley R-4374A (California only) Center (automatic transmission): Holley R-4376A (49-state), Holley R-4144A (California only) Rear: Holley R-4383A (49-state), Holley R-4365A (California only)
Pistons	Cast-aluminum alloy
Compression ratio	10.5:1
Crankshaft	Drop-forged steel
Valves	2.08 inches (intake), 1.74 inches (exhaust)
Valve lifters	Hydraulic

Engines

Exhaust system	Dual
Horsepower (factory advertised)	390 at 4,700 rpm
Torque (factory advertised)	490 ft-lbs at 3,200 rpm
Fuel required	Premium
Optional 426 Hemi	
Displacement	426 ci
Bore and stroke	4.25 x 3.75 inches
Carburetion, 2x4-barrel	Front: Carter AFB-4742S (50-state) Rear: Carter AFB-4745S (4-speed) or Carter AFB-4746S (automatic) (50-state)
Pistons	Forged-aluminum alloy
Compression ratio	10.2:1
Crankshaft	Drop-forged steel
Valves	2.25 inches (intake) 1.94 inches (exhaust)
Valve lifters	Hydraulic (replaced solid lifters for 1970)
Horsepower (factory advertised)	425 at 5,000 rpm
Torque (factory advertised)	490 ft-lbs at 4,000 rpm
Fuel required	Premium

Transmissions

Standard Chrysler 3-Speed Manual	
Fully synchronized	Yes (new for 1970 on Chrysler 3-speeds)
Gear ratios	2.55 (1st), 1.49 (2nd), 1.00 (3rd)
Available rear-axle ratios	3.23, 3.55*, 3.91*
Shifter	Floor-mounted stick

* With Sure Grip differential only.

Optional Chrysler/New Process Gear 4-Speed Manual (with 23-Spline Input Shaft)	
Fully synchronized	Yes
Gear ratios	2.47 (1st), 1.77 (2nd), 1.34 (3rd), 1.00 (4th)
Available rear-axle ratios	3.23, 3.55*, 3.91*
Shifter	Floor- or console-mounted stick with Hurst Pistol Grip shifter handle

* With Sure Grip differential only.

Optional Chrysler/New Process Gear 4-Speed Manual (Heavy-Duty "Hemi" 4-Speed With 18-Spline Input Shaft)	
Fully synchronized	Yes
Gear ratios	2.44 (1st), 1.77 (2nd), 1.34 (3rd), 1.00 (4th)
Available rear-axle ratios	3.23, 3.55*, 3.54* (Hemi and 440 Six Barrel only), 3.91*, 4.10*
Shifter	Floor- or console-mounted stick with Hurst Pistol Grip shifter handle and knob

* With Sure Grip differential only.

Transmissions

Optional Chrysler TorqueFlite Automatic

Forward speeds	3
Gear lever	Steering-column mounted (standard), console mounted (optional)
Gear ratios	2.45:1 (1st), 1.45:1 (2nd), 1.00 (3rd)
Available rear-axle ratios	3.23, 3.55 (383 only), 3.54 (Hemi and 440 Six Barrel only), 3.91*, 4.10*
* With Sure Grip differential only.	

Rear-Axle Assemblies

Standard	Chrysler-built with 8¾-inch ring gear, Sure Grip limited-slip differential optional
Optional (with Track Pak and Super Track Pak)	Dana-built Dana 60 with 9¾-inch ring gear, Sure Grip limited-slip differential optional

Brakes

Standard	Four-wheel drum-and-shoe brakes with 11-inch-diameter drums, non–power assisted
Optional	Front disc brakes (power brakes required) Power brakes, vacuum assisted

Steering

Standard	Chrysler-built recirculating ball, 5.3 turns lock-to-lock, non–power assisted
Optional	Chrysler-built recirculating ball with power assist, 3.5 turns lock-to-lock

Suspension

Front	Longitudinal torsion bars, unequal-length A-Arms and heavy-duty shock absorbers, plus .94-inch-diameter front sway bar Torsion bar with 383, 41 inches (length) x .90 inch (diameter) Torsion bar with 440 Six Barrel or 426 Hemi, 41 inches (length) x .92 inch (diameter)
Rear	Asymmetrical leaf springs Standard, five leaves per side, with heavy-duty shock absorbers Optional (required with 440 Six Barrel and 426 Hemi), five leaves per side, plus two half-leaves on the passenger's side for 440 Six Barrel and 426 Hemi; heavy-duty shock absorbers

Wheels and Tires

Wheels

Standard	14 x 6–inch stamped steel, painted body color, with Plymouth hubcap
Optional	14-inch Deluxe wheel cover or wire wheel cover; 14 x 5½–inch five-spoke "Magnum" road wheels; 14 x 5½–inch or 15 x 7–inch Rallye road wheels

Tires

Standard	F70-14 fiberglass-belted bias-ply, white sidewall
Optional	F70-14 fiberglass-belted bias-ply, raised white letter F60-15 fiberglass-belted bias-ply, raised white letter

APPENDIX B

EXTERIOR COLORS

Standard Colors

Color	Code
Black Velvet	TX9
Alpine White	EW1
Blue Fire Metallic	EB5
Jamaica Blue Metallic	EB7
Lime Green Metallic	FF4
Ivy Green Metallic	EF8
Deep Burnt Orange Metallic	FK5
Yellow Gold	DY3
Sandpebble Beige	BL1
Rally Red	FE5
Burnt Tan Metallic	FT6
Citron Mist Metallic	FY4
Ice Blue Metallic	EB3

Extra-Cost Optional High-Impact Colors

Color	Code
In Violet*	FC7
Tor Red*	EV2
Lime Light*	FJ5
Vitamin C Orange*	EK2
Lemon Twist*	FY1
Sassy Grass Green**	FJ6
Moulin Rouge**	FM3

*Available throughout the 1970 model year.
** Added in February 1970.

Vinyl Tops

Color	Code
Black	V1X
White	V1W
Green	V1F
"Gator Grain" Black	V1G

Convertible Tops

Color	Code
Black	V3X
White	V3W

Striping and Accents

Optional Transverse Rear Stripe

Available on hardtop, convertible, or coupe with A87.

Color	Code
Black	V8X
White	V8W
Gold	V8Y

Optional Code V6Y Dust Trail Side Stripes

Available on all models.

Reflective Gold (aft of the at-speed cartoon Road Runner decal on each front fender, extending rearward to the simulated scoop on the quarter panel).

Optional Code V21 Performance Hood Paint

Available on all models.

Matte Black

INTERIOR COLORS

For two-color interiors, the first color is on the seats, door panels, and rear-seat side panels; the second color is on the carpets, dashboard, steering column, and hardtop/coupe headliners.

Standard

On coupe all-vinyl front/rear-bench-seat interior with black rubber floor mats.

Color	Code
Black	M2X9
Blue	M2B5
Tan	M2T5

On hardtop/convertible all-vinyl front/rear-bench-seat interior with color-keyed nylon loop-pile carpeting (included with A87 Decor Group on coupe).

Color	Code
Blue	H2B5
Green*	H2F8
Burnt Orange	H2K4
Black	H2X9
Tan*	H2T5
White and Blue	H2BW
White and Burnt Orange	H2KW
White and Black	H2XW
* NA on convertibles.	

On all-vinyl front-bucket/rear-bench-seat interior, with color-keyed nylon loop-pile carpeting.

Color	Code	Color	Code
Blue	P6B5	Gold and Black	P6XY
Green*	P6F8	White and Black	P6XW
Burnt Orange	P6K4	White and Burnt Orange	P6KW
Charcoal and Black	P6XA	White and Blue	P6BW
Tan*	P6T5		

* NA on convertibles.

APPENDIX D
PRICES

These MSRPs are as of September 23, 1969, the day the 1970 Plymouths went on sale.

Road Runner, V-8

Code	Model	Price
RM21	2-door coupe	2,896
RM23	2-door hardtop	3,034
RM27	convertible	3,289

Accessory Group

Code	Package	Price
A01	Light Package (fender-mounted turn indicators, trunk light, glove-box light, map/courtesy light, ashtray light, time-delay ignition light)	29.60
A04	Basic Group (solid-state AM radio, power steering, remote-control outside mirror, driver's side)	177.20
A87	Road Runner Decor Group (coupe only): custom-style vinyl trim (H2 or P6 trims only), B-pillar molding, bright armrest bases, three-spoke steering wheel with partial horn ring, bright door panels, transverse tape stripe	81.50
A35	Trailer Towing Package (NA with Hemi or 440 Six Barrel engines)	14.05

Comfort and Convenience

Code	Description	Price
C16	Center console	54.45
C92	Accessory floor mats	13.60
G31	Mirror, manual, RH outside	6.85
G33	Mirror, remote control, LH outside	10.45
J21	Electric clock	18.45
L42	Headlight time delay and warning signal	18.20
N88	Automatic Speed Control (TorqueFlite only; NA Hemi, 440 Six Barrel, or with Air Grabber hood)	57.95

Electrical

Code	Description	Price
F11	50-ampere alternator (standard with A/C on V-8 cars)	11.00
F25	70-amp/hour battery (standard with Hemi and 440 engines)	12.95

Engine

Code	Description	Price
E63	383 Magnum V-8 4-barrel	Standard
E74	426 Hemi V-8 2x4–barrel*	841.05
E87	440 Six Barrel V-8*	249.55

*NA with air conditioning, speed control, or 3-speed manual transmission; 12-month or 12,000-mile powertrain warranty applies in place of standard 5-year/50,000-mile warranty and only applies to the car's first owner.

Glass, Tinted

Code	Description	Price
G11	All windows (except convertible rear window)	40.70
G15	Windshield only	26.25

Heating and Cooling

Code	Description	Price
H51	Airtemp air conditioning with heater (NA with Air Grabber, 440 Six Barrel, or Hemi)	357.65
H31	Rear window defogger (NA with convertible)	26.25

Miscellaneous Description

Code	Description	Price
J55	Undercoating and hood insulator pad	16.60
N95	Evaporative emissions control (required on all cars registered in California; NA otherwise)	37.85
N97	Noise reduction package (required in California for all 383-4 Barrel and 440 engines)	No charge

Moldings and Bumper Guards

Code	Description	Price
M05	Door-edge guards	4.65
M25	Custom sill molding	21.15
M31	Belt line molding (standard on convertibles; NA with Dust Trail stripe)	13.60
M83	Bumper guards, rear	16.00

Paint and Stripes

Code	Description	Price
V6Y	Dust Trail side tape stripe	15.55
	High Impact paint	14.05
	Two-tone paint (NA convertible)	23.30
V21	Performance hood paint	18.05

Performance and Suspension

Code	Description	Price
A31	High-performance axle package (383 4-barrel only; NA with 3-speed manual transmission, A/C, or trailer-towing package)	102.15

A32 Super Performance Axle Package*

Code	Description	Price
440	With automatic transmission only	250.65
426	Hemi with automatic transmission only	221.40

NA with A/C or trailer towing

A33 Track Pak*

Description	Price
Hemi or 440 with 4-speed	142.85

Includes 3.54-geared Dana 60 rear end; NA with A/C

A34 Super Track Pak*

Description	Price
Hemi or 440 with 4-speed	235.65

Includes 4.10-geared Dana 60 rear end; NA with A/C

A36 Performance Axle Package*

Description	Price
With 383 with 4-speed or TorqueFlite	102.15
With 440 and automatic only	92.25
With Hemi and TorqueFlite only	64.40

NA with trailer towing

D91 Sure Grip Differential*

Code	Description	Price
J45	Hood hold-down pins	15.40
N42	Bright exhaust trumpets (standard with Hemi; NA in California)	20.80
N85	Tachometer (includes clock)	68.45
N96	Air Grabber hood (standard with Hemi; NA with A/C or speed control)	65.55
S13	Heavy-duty suspension	Standard
S15	Extra-heavy-duty handling package (standard with Hemi & 440 engines)	No charge
S25	Heavy-duty shock absorbers	Standard
Available only in A33/A34 Track Paks with 426 Hemi with 4-speed manual transmission		42.35

Power Equipment and Brakes

Code	Description	Price
B11	Heavy-duty (drum) brakes	Standard
B41	Disc brakes, front (power brakes required)	27.90
B51	Power brakes	42.95
P31	Power windows (NA coupe)	105.20

Power Equipment and Brakes

S77	Power steering	105.20

Radios Without A04 Basic Group

Code	Description	Price
R11	Solid-state AM	61.55
R21	Solid-state AM/FM (Monaural)	134.95
R22	Solid-state AM with stereo tape player	196.25

Radios with A04 Basic Group

Code	Description	Price
R21	Solid-state AM/FM (Monaural)	73.50
R22	Solid-state AM with stereo tape player	134.75
R31	Rear-seat speaker (NA convertible)	14.05

Seating

Code	Description	Price
C55	Bucket seats, Vinyl	100.85
C21	Center seat cushion and folding armrest (with bucket seats; NA with C16 Console)	54.45
C62	Six-way "Comfort Position" driver-side seat adjuster (with bucket seats only)	33.30

Seat/Shoulder Belts

Code	Description	Price
C13	Front shoulder belts (convertible only)	26.45
C14	Rear shoulder belts (NA convertible)	26.45
C15	Seat belts, deluxe	13.75

Steering Wheels Without A55 or A87

Code	Description	Price
S81	Three-spoke wood-grain steering wheel (NA with S83)	
RR	Coupe	32.10
	Hardtop and convertible	26.75
S83	Two-spoke rim-blow steering wheel (NA with S81)	
	Coupe	29.00
	Hardtop and convertible	19.15

Steering Wheels with A55 or A87

Code	Description	Price
S81	Three-spoke wood-grain steering wheel (NA with S83), coupe	26.75
S83	Two-spoke rim-blow steering wheel (NA with S81), coupe	16.05

Transmissions		
Code	Description	Price
D13	3-speed manual floor shifter (NA with A35 trailer towing package)	Standard
D21	4-speed manual with Hurst Pistol Grip shifter (NA with trailer towing; A33 or A34 required with Hemi or 440 engines)	197.25
D34	TorqueFlite automatic	227.05

Wheels and Wheel Covers		
Code	Description	Price
W11	Deluxe wheel covers, 14 inches	21.30
W15	Wire wheel covers, 14 inches	64.10
W21	Rallye Road wheels, 14 or 15 inches	43.10
W23	Chrome-styled road wheels (Five-Spoke), 14 inches	86.15

Tires		
Code	Description	Price
T87	F70-14 RWL	No Charge
U84	F60-15 RWL (S15 required with 383); replaces standard F70-14 WSW	63.25

APPENDIX E

FENDER TAG DECODING

In 1970, Chrysler affixed a metal tag to the driver-side front fenderwell, under the hood, of each passenger car. It documented the engine, transmission, exterior and interior color and trim codes, optional equipment, and any special-order (non-regular-production) equipment that was factory installed.

Fender-tag codes used by Chrysler Corporation in 1970 included the following. This list is courtesy of MyMopar.com.

Code	Description	Code	Description
A01	**Light Package**	A21	Elastomeric Colored Front Bumper Package
A02	Driver Aid Group	A22	Elastomeric Colored Front and Rear Bumper Package
A03	Town & Country Group	A24	Trunk & Spare Tire Dress-Up
A04	**Basic (Radio) Group**	**A31**	**High Performance Axle Package with 3.91 Ratio**
A07	Turnpike Package	**A32**	**Super Performance Axle Package with 4.10 Ratio**
A12	Chrysler 300 Hurst	**A33**	**Track Pak with 3.54 Ratio**
A13	**Plymouth Road Runner Superbird**	**A34**	**Super Track Pak with 4.10 Ratio**
A14	Spring Special Package	**A35**	**H.D. Trailer Towing Package**

Bold signifies use on the Road Runner.

Code	Description
A36	**Performance Axle Package with 3.55 Ratio**
A37	Taxi Package
A38	Police Package
A44	Rear Window Louver Package
A45	Front & Rear Spoiler Package
A46	Molding Package
A47	Special Edition Package
A48	Dress Up Package
A51	Sport Fury S-23
A52	Sport Fury GT
A53	Trans-Am Package ('Cuda AAR/Challenger T/A)
A54	Colored Bumper Package
A55	Custom Trim Package
A62	Rallye Instrument Cluster Package
A63	Challenger Molding Group
A65	Dart GT Package
A66	Challenger 340 Performance Package
A67	Backlight Louver Package
A73	Special Value Package, XH29 Charger
A82	Police Ornamentation Group
A83	New York Taxi Package
A87	**Road Runner Decor Package**
A88	Interior Decor Group
A91	Western Sport Special
A93	B & E Body Coupe Package
A94	Gold Duster Special Package
A95	Chrysler Spring Special
A97	Fury Spring Special A
A98	Fury Spring Special B
B11	H.D. Drum Brakes, 10 inches, Auto Adjusting (A-Body)
B11	**H.D. Drum Brakes, 11 inches, Auto Adjusting (B+C+E Body)**
B31	**H.D. Drum Brakes, 11 inches, Manual Adjusting (B+C Body)**
B41	**Front Disc Brakes with Standard 10-inch Rear Drum**
B42	**Front Disc Brakes with H.D. 11-inch Rear Drum**
B51	**Power Brakes**
B61	Brakes, Standard Drum

Code	Description
C04	**Seat Belts, Delete All Standard**
C13	**Front Shoulder Belts**
C14	**Rear Shoulder Belts**
C15	**Deluxe Seat Belts**
C16	**Console with Wood-Grain Panel**
C21	**Center Front Seat Cushion**
C22	Armrest Base-Painted
C23	Rear Armrests with Ashtray
C26	Consolette with Formed Headlining
C32	Delete Head Restraints
C34	Front Seat Shield
C37D	**Richard Petty Blue (Special Order Paint)**
C51	Bench Seat-Split 50/50
C55	**Bucket Seats**
C61	Bucket Seat Left Reclining
C62	**Left-Hand Six Way Adjustable Bucket Seat**
C65	Air Foam Front Seat
C71	Air Foam Front & Rear Seat
C81	Seat Spring, H.D. Front
C83	Seat Spring, H.D. Rear
C85	Seat Spring, H.D. Front & Rear
C91	Floor Mats, H.D. Front
C92	**Floor Mats, Accessory Rubber**
C93	**Carpet**
C95	Floor Mats, H.D. Front & Rear Black
C96	Trunk Dress-Up Partial
C97	Trunk Dress-Up
CTD	**Codes Continued on Second Fender Tag**
D11	3-Speed Manual Transmission-Column Shift 6-Cylinder
D12	3-Speed Manual Transmission-Column Shift 8-Cylinder
D13	**3-Speed Manual Transmission-Floor Shift**
D21	**4-Speed Manual Transmission**
D31	A904 3-Speed Automatic Transmission
D32	**Heavy-Duty Automatic Transmission**
D34	Light-Duty Automatic Transmission
D36	A-727 3-Speed Automatic Transmission
D41	Clutch H.D. 9½-inch Diameter

Bold signifies use on the Road Runner.

Code	Description
D49	Special Order Transmission
D51	**2.76:1 Rear-Axle Ratio**
D53	**3.23:1 Rear-Axle Ratio**
D55	**2.45:1 Rear-Axle Ratio**
D56	**3.54:1 Rear-Axle Ratio**
D57	**3.91:1 Rear-Axle Ratio**
D58	**4.10:1 Rear-Axle Ratio**
D69	**Special Order Rear Axle**
D91	**Sure Grip Differential**
E22	198 ci, 1-barrel, 6-cylinder, 125 hp
E24	225 ci, 1-barrel, 6-cylinder, 145 hp
E25	225 ci, 1-barrel, 6-cylinder, H.D. 145 hp
E44	318 ci, 2-barrel, V-8, 230 hp
E55	340 ci, 4-barrel, V-8, 275 hp
E55	340 ci, 3x2-barrel, V-8, 290 hp
E61	383 ci, 2-barrel, V-8, 290 hp
E63	**383 ci, 4-barrel, V-8, H.P. 335 hp**
E74	**426 Hemi, 2x4-barrel, V-8, 425 hp**
E85	440 ci, 4-barrel, V-8, 350 hp
E86	440 ci, 4-barrel, V-8 (High Performance), 375 hp
E87	**440 ci, 3x2-barrel, V-8 (High Performance), 390 hp**
E91	Police Engine
END	**End of Sales Codes**
EN1	**End of Sales Codes, Assembly Line 1**
EN2	**End of Sales Codes, Assembly Line 2**
F01	440 ci, 4-barrel police engine conversion package
F08	Trans-Am Engine (340 "TA" block and heads plus 3x2–barrel carburetors)
F11	**Alternator, 50-amp**
F13	**Alternator, 60-amp**
F15	**Alternator, 65-amp**
F17	Radio Suppresion Package
F22	**Battery, 46-amp-hour (Series 24 with Green Caps)**
F23	**Battery, 59-amp-hour (Series 24 with Yellow Caps)**
F25	**Battery, 70-amp-hour (Series 27 with Red Caps)**
F56	**Antifreeze Tested -35° F**
F95	Certified Speedometer
F96	**Oil Pressure Gauge**
G11	**Tinted Glass (All)**

Code	Description
G12	**Tinted Side Glass**
G15	**Tinted Windshield**
G18	**Clear Windshield (with Air Conditioning)**
G21	**Clear Glass (with Air Conditioning)**
G24	Omit Vent Windows
G25	Add Vent Windows
G30	**Delete Mirrors**
G31	**OS RH Manual Standard Mirror**
G32	**OS RH Manual Racing Mirror**
G33	**OS LH Remote Standard Mirror**
G34	**OS LH Remote Racing Mirror**
G35	**Delete Standard Outside Mirror**
G36	OS Dual Racing Mirrors
G41	**Day/Night Inside Rearview Mirror**
G42	Non-Day/Night Inside Rearview Mirror
H11	**Heater**
H25	**Heater Delete**
H31	**Rear Window Defogger**
H51	**Airtemp Air Conditioning, Single Unit, Manual Temperature Control**
H52	Airtemp Air Conditioning, Single Unit, Automatic Temperature Control
H53	Airtemp Air Conditioning, Dual Unit, Manual Temperature Control
H54	Airtemp Air Conditioning, Dual Unit, Automatic Temperature Control
J01	**Driver Education Decals (on Front Doors)**
J11	**Glove Box Lock**
J15	**Cigar Lighter**
J21	**Electric Clock**
J25	**Three-Speed Wipers**
J26	Tailgate Window Wiper/Washer
J31	Dual Horns
J32	Single Horn
J41	**Pedal Dress-Up**
J45	**Hood Tie-Down Pins**
J46	**Locking Gas Cap**
J54	**Sport Hood**
J55	**Undercoating with Hood Pad**

Bold signifies use on the Road Runner.

Code	Description	Code	Description
J64	Instrument Panel Wood Grain	M73	Front and Rear Colored Bumpers
J68	Backlight Louvers	**M81**	**Front Bumper Guards**
J78	Front Spoiler	**M83**	**Rear Bumper Guards**
J81	Rear Spoiler, Wing Type	M84	Tail Step Sill Plate
J82	Rear Spoiler, Ducktail Type	M85	Front and Rear Bumper Guards
L05	Map Light	M88	Decklid Moldings Treatment
L06	Dome/Reading Lamp	M91	Luggage Rack
L11	**Glove Box Light**	M93	Body-Side Moldings Delete
L15	**Ash Receiver Lamp**	N25	Engine Block Heater
L25	**Trunk Lamp**	N31	Optional Engine Compression Ratio
L31	**Hood/Fender-Mounted Turn Signals**	**N41**	**Dual Exhaust**
L34	Road Lights	**N42**	**Chrome Exhaust Tips**
L35	Cornering Lamps	N44	Side Exhaust
L42	Headlamp Time Delay	N45	High-Capacity Fan
L61	Dome Lamp Switch Rear Doors	N46	Medium-Capacity Fan
L65	**Ignition Switch Lamp with Time Delay**	**N51**	**Maximum Engine Cooling**
L68	Auto Headlamp Dimmer	**N65**	**Seven-Blade Torque Drive Fan**
L71	Door Ajar Lamp	N75	Auxiliary Transmission Fluid Cooler
L72	Headlamp On Buzzer	N81	Fast Idle Control
L73	Seatbelt Unfastened Lamp	**N85**	**Tachometer**
L75	Low Fuel Lamp	**N88**	**Automatic Speed Control**
L76	Heater Controls Lamp	N94	Fiberglass Fresh Air Hood
M05	**Door-Edge Moldings**	**N95**	**Emissions Control Package (California only)**
M21	**Roof Drip-Rail Moldings**	**N96**	**Fresh Air Hood (Air Grabber)**
M25	**Wide Sill moldings**	**N97**	**Noise Reduction Package (California only)**
M26	**Wheel Lip Moldings**	P21	Power Front Bench Seat
M27	**Delete Wheel Lip Moldings**	P25	Power Left Front Seat
M28	Front Bumper Periphery	P28	Power Left/Right Front Seat
M31	Belt Moldings	**P31**	**Power Windows**
M33	Body-Side Moldings	P33	Power Vent Windows
M38	Decklid Finish Panel Moldings	P35	Power Tailgate Window
M41	**License Plate Frame**	**P37**	**Power Convertible Top**
M42	Front Stone Shield Moldings	P41	Power Door Locks
M43	Grille Trim Moldings	P45	Power Decklid Release
M44	Hood and Fender Moldings	**R11**	**AM Radio (2 Watts)**
M46	Simulated Quarter-Panel Scoops	R13	Deluxe AM Radio (5½ Watts)
M51	Power Sunroof with Vinyl Roof	**R21**	**AM/FM Radio (5½ Watts)**
M71	Front Colored Bumper	**R22**	**AM Radio with 8-Track (10 Watts)**
M72	Rear Colored Bumper	R23	Search Tune AM/FM Radio (5½ Watts)

Bold signifies use on the Road Runner.

Code	Description
R31	**Rear Seat Speaker(s)**
R32	Dual Rear Speakers
R35	AM/FM Stereo Radio (10 Watts)
R37	AM/FM Stereo with 8-Track
R45	Oversize Manual Antenna
R48	Power Antenna
S11	Suspension, heavy-duty without Sway Bar
S13	**Suspension, heavy-duty with Sway Bar**
S15	**Hemi Suspension with Sway Bar**
S17	Reduced Rate Suspension
S25	**Firm Ride Shocks, 1-Inch Front and Rear**
S28	**Firm Ride Shocks, 1-Inch Front and 1⅜-Inch Rear**
S31	**Front Sway Bar**
S61	Tilt/Telescopic Steering Column
S62	Tilt Steering Column
S74	Quick Ratio Power Steering
S76	Steering Wheel Horn Ring Full/Fleet
S77	**Power Steering**
S78	Full Horn Ring
S79	**Lower 1/2 Horn Ring**
S81	**Premium Wood-Grain Steering Wheel**
S83	**Rim-Blow Wood-Grain Steering Wheel**
T86	**F70-14 White Sidewall**
T87	**F70-14 Raised White Letter**
U01	E60-15 Raised White Letter (Front)
U01	G60-15 Raised White Letter (Rear)
U82	E60-15 Raised White Letter, Goodyear Polyglas
U83	**F60-15 Raised White Letter, Goodyear Polyglas**
V01	**Mono-Tone Paint Treatment**
V02	**Two-Tone Paint Treatment**
V08	**Paint, Trim, and Vinyl Roof Edit Waiver**
V09	**Paint Special Order**
V1*	**Full Vinyl Top**
* Missing digit represents these color choices:	
A	Gunmetal
B	Blue
C	Black Alligator
F	**Green**
G	**Black Gator Grain**

Bold signifies use on the Road Runner.

Code	Description
J	Walnut Pattern
K	Walnut
L	Champagne
L	Parchment
M	Burgundy
P	Mod Yellow (Barracuda only)
Q	Mod Blue (Barracuda only)
T	Tan
W	**White**
X	**Black**
Y	Gold
Y	Tortoise Grain
9	*Special Order (V19 = Black on Superbird)*
V21	**Performance Hood Treatment**
V22	**Delete Sport Hood Treatment**
V23	Paint Delete Body Side
V24	Performance Hood Treatment with engine displacement number
V3*	**Convertible Top**
* Missing digit represents these color choices:	
w	**White**
X	**Black**
9	**Special Order**
V4*	70 Body Side Stripe (Strobe Tape)
* Missing digit represents these color choices:	
J	*Lime Daylight Fluorescent*
M	*Pink Daylight Fluorescent*
W	*White*
X	*Black*
V5*	Body Side Molding
V6*	Longitudinal Stripes
V7*	Accent Stripes
V8*	Transverse Stripes
V9*	Bumble Bee Stripes
* Missing digit represents these color choices:	
A	*Gunmetal*
B	*Light Blue*
C	*In Violet*
D	*Dark Blue*
E	*Bright Red*

Code	Description
F	Green
H	Trans-Am Black
J	Chartreuse
K	Go Mango Orange
M	Magenta
R	Red
T	Tan
V	Orange
W	White
X	Black
Y	Yellow
3	Delete
W11	Deluxe Wheel Covers
W13	Deep Dish Wheel Covers
W15	Wire Wheel Covers
W18	**Simulated Mag Wheel Covers**
W21	**Rallye Wheels**
W23	**Road Wheels**
W34	**Collapsible Spare Tire**
Y05	**Build to USA Specs**

Code	Description
Y07	**Build to Canada Specs**
Y09	**Build to Specs for Export**
Y11	**Domestic Publications ("Press car" furnished to magazine/newspaper writers for road testing)**
Y13	**Dealer Demonstrator**
Y14	**Sold Car (ordered by dealer to customer's order)**
Y15	**Direct Sale (sold directly by Chrysler)**
Y16	**Sales Bank (Chrysler's new-car inventory, held at or near the assembly plants)**
Y17	**Corporate Lease Car System**
Y22	**Corporate Lease Car-Executive**
Y28	**Company Car/Public Relations**
Y33	**Fleet Sales**
Y39	**Special Order**
Y54	**Chrysler Management Employee Purchase**
Y91	**Show Car Finish A, Less Gas**
Y92	**Show Car Finish B, Less Gas**
Y93	**71 Show Car Finish B, Less Gas**
Y97	**70 Show Car Finish with 3 Gallons Gas**

CHRYSLER PASSENGER CAR VIN CODES

The following 1970 information is from lhmopar.com.

DECODING YOUR VIN

VIN Character	Designation
1, 2	RM represents Road Runner Model
3, 4	Body Type
	RM21, Coupe
	RM23, Hardtop
	RM27, Convertible
5	Engine
	N, 383 High-Performance
	R, 426 Hemi
	T, 440 High-Performance

VIN Character	Designation
	V, 440-6
6	Year
	0
7	Assembly Plant
	A, Lynch Road, Michigan
	E, Los Angeles, California
	G, St. Louis, Missouri
8 to 13	Individual Model Identification

First Digit	Car Line
B	Plymouth Barracuda, 'Cuda, and AAR 'Cuda
C	Chrysler Newport, 300, and New Yorker
D	Dodge Polara, Polara 500, and Monaco
J	Dodge Challenger, Challenger R/T, and Challenger T/A
L	Dodge Dart, Swinger, and Swinger 340
P	Plymouth Fury I, Fury II, Fury III, Sport Fury, and Fury Gran Coupe
R	Plymouth Belvedere, Satellite, Sport Satellite, Road Runner, and GTX
V	Plymouth Valiant, Duster, and Duster 340
W	Dodge Coronet Deluxe, Coronet 440, Coronet 500, and Coronet R/T
X	Dodge Charger, Charger 500, and Charger R/T
Y	Imperial Crown and LeBaron
Second Digit	**Price Class**
E	Economy
L	Low
M	Medium
H	High
P	Premium
S	Special
K	Police
T	Taxi
N	New York Taxi
Third and Fourth Digits	**Body Style**
21	2-door sedan or coupe
23	2-door hardtop
27	Convertible
29	2-door sports hardtop
41	4-door sedan
43	4-door hardtop
45	6-passenger station wagon
46	9-passenger station wagon
Fifth Digit	**Engine**
B	198 1x1 barrel 6-cylinder G engine
C	225 1x1 barrel 6-cylinder RG engine
E	Special Order 6-cylinder engine
G	318 1x2 barrel 8-cylinder LA engine
H	340 1x4 barrel 8-cylinder LA engine (High Performance)
J	340 3x2 barrel 8-cylinder LA engine (High Performance)
K	360 1x2 barrel 8-cylinder LA engine
L	383 1x2 barrel 8-cylinder B engine

N	383 1x4 barrel 8-cylinder B engine (High Performance)
R	426 2x4 barrel 8-cylinder RB engine (Hemi)
T	440 1x4 barrel 8-cylinder RB engine
U	440 1x4 barrel 8-cylinder RB engine (High Performance)
V	440 3x2 barrel 8-cylinder RB engine (High Performance)
Z	Special Order 8-cylinder engine

Sixth Digit	Model Year
0	1970

Seventh Digit	Assembly Plant
A	Lynch Road, Detroit, Michigan
B	Hamtramck, Michigan
C	Jefferson Avenue, Detroit, Michigan
D	Belvidere, Illinois
E	Los Angeles, California
F	Newark, Delaware
G	St. Louis, Missouri
H	New Stanton, Pennsylvania
R	Windsor, Ontario, Canada

Eighth through Thirteenth Digits

The remaining six digits indicate the build-sequence number (serial number) at that assembly plant, typically starting with 100001. This number included all cars built at that plant during that year, not just the car line represented by the VIN.

The following example from Henry Liebman's Road Runner Convertible is the information found on the fender tag.

This photograph shows a 1970 Plymouth Road Runner's fender tag. On it, along with the VIN (RM27N0G), are codes for the factory-installed colors, features, and options, as well as when and where it was built and in what order it moved down the assembly line. Reading it from left to right, beginning with the bottom line, it is decoded as follows:

R	Midsize Plymouth		0	Model year (1970)
M	Price code (M is for Road Runner)		G	Assembly plant code (G is for St Louis, where all Road Runner convertibles were built)
7	Body style (Convertible)			
N	Engine code (Road Runner 383 V-8)			

00474 Build-sequence number at St. Louis Assembly for 1970 model year, starting with 10001.

E63	Road Runner 383-ci V-8
D32	TorqueFlite automatic transmission
FK5	Deep Burnt Orange Metallic paint
H2XW	White and Burnt Orange interior trim
EW1	White interior door frames (color painted on inside of doors at factory to match door upholstery)
305	Date of final assembly (March 5, 1970)
C08016	Order number
V3W	White convertible top
A01	Light Package
G31	OS RH manual standard mirror
G33	OS LH remote standard mirror
J25	3-speed electric windshield wipers and washers

J45	Hood tie-down pins
L31	Hood/fender-mounted turn signals (hood mounted on this car, at aft end of hood bulge)
M25	Wide sill moldings
M31	Belt moldings
N85	Tachometer
N96	Air Grabber hood
P31	Power windows
R22	Radio push-button AM with 8-track tape player
V8W	Transverse rear stripe, white
Y07	Built to Canada specifications
END	End of sales codes

APPENDIX G

PRODUCTION DATA

The following 1970 production totals are from MyMopar.com.

Coupe (RM21)	
383/3-speed	1,330
383/TorqueFlite	6,888
383/4-speed	5,839
440 Six Barrel/TorqueFlite	222
440 Six Barrel/4-speed	429
426 Hemi/TorqueFlite	30
426 Hemi/4-speed	44

Note: Plus seven 4-speeds and seven TorqueFlites exported to Canada; "not included by transmission in totals."

Hardtop (RM23)	
383/3-speed	584
383/TorqueFlite	11,639
383/4-speed	7,993

440 Six Barrel/TorqueFlite	43:
440 Six Barrel/4-speed	69;
426 Hemi/TorqueFlite	16
426 Hemi/4-speed	59

Note: Plus six 4-speeds and six TorqueFlites exported to Canada; "not included by transmission in totals."

Convertible (RM41)	
383/3-speed	13
383/TorqueFlite	429
383/4-speed	179
440 Six Barrel/TorqueFlite	14
440 Six Barrel/4-speed	20
426 Hemi/TorqueFlite	2
426 Hemi/4-speed	1